Earthquakes

Don DeNevi

with an introduction by Peter L. Ward, Seismologist

CELESTIAL ARTS
Millbrae, California

Cover design by Betsy Bruno
Diagrams by Jack Popovich

Published by CELESTIAL ARTS, 231 Adrian Road,
Millbrae, California 94030

First printing: May, 1977
Manufactured in the United States of America

Library of Congress Cataloging in Publication Data

DeNevi, Donald P.
    Earthquakes

    Bibliography: p.
    Includes index.
    1. Earthquakes.   I.   Title.
QE534.2.D46   551.2'2   77-8507
ISBN: 0-89087-148-5

1 2 3 4 5 6 7 8   82 81 80 79 78 77

Table of Contents

DEDICATION

This book is dedicated to
San Francisco architect, Aaron Green, F.A.I.A.,
whose methods of flexible, organic construction
could save countless lives during earthquakes

Introduction

A fundamental belief in our religion and philosophy is that the ground beneath us is firm, immovable—the stable base of our lives. Thus, it is not surprising that so many people feel deep terror when the ground suddenly shakes violently in an earthquake—destroying buildings, snuffing out lives, changing the course of rivers. For centuries man explained these events as punishments from God or the gods for sins. Some cultures believed earthquakes were caused by monstrous animals with mystical powers.

Scientists studying earthquakes, especially over the last century, are finding that such events are not so mystical— there are reasons for earthquakes. There are places in the world where their occurrence is inevitable, and there are areas where they do not occur at all. Some of the most exciting work in the last decade suggests that someday large earthquakes will be reliably predicted years in advance and might even be controlled. With proper city planning and architectural design, earthquakes can be planned for and their damaging effects minimized.

This book provides a very readable introduction to the awesome power of earthquakes, what earthquakes are, why they happen, and what the effects of earthquakes are likely to be. Even more important, this book outlines how we can plan to reduce the damage and loss of life from earthquakes and what the state of the art of earthquake prediction is. This is a valuable primer for anyone who lives in earthquake country, which as you shall find, includes many of the most populated areas of the world.

Peter L. Ward

Peter Ward, Chief, Branch of Earthquake Mechanics and Prediction, U.S Geological Survey.

Preface

During the next decade, it is possible that thousands of lives will be lost in major earthquakes. Most of the unfortunate victims will be killed as non-earthquake-resistant dwellings collapse along America's various active seismic faults. Timely warnings of the impending temblors advising citizens to either remain indoors or seek safety from dangerous buildings out-of-doors until the devastation is over will undoubtedly save the lives of tens of thousands. The purpose of this book is to present a simple, easy-to-understand evaluation of the current state of seismology and its ability to predict earthquakes and reduce hazards.

Throughout man's complex history, prediction and control have always been connected to myth, folklore, sorcery, and even charlatanism. Today, the investigation of earthquakes is a rapidly growing science. A lively and fascinating study, seismology, the science of earthquakes and related phenomena, has brought about a revolution in ideas about the behavior of the earth's surface. Formerly, most scientists regarded the earth as rigid and the continents as fixed. Now, the earth's surface is seen as slowly deformable and the continents as "rafts" floating on a "sea" of denser rock. While the continents have repeatedly collided and joined together, they also are breaking up and separating in different patterns, probably growing larger in the process. The widespread acceptance of the continental drift concept has transformed the earth sciences.

Nothing can be done to stop the motion of the continents; the plate under California will continue to experience earthquakes in the future, just as it has for millions of years. At long intervals, great disasters can be expected, but none of them more cataclysmic than those of the past. Although earthquakes cannot be stopped, recent work has opened the possibility of not only predicting them, but artificially triggering smaller quakes to release energy instead of allowing it to be stored up and cause more powerful shocks.

The following pages are an attempt to present the latest information on this critically important and dynamic science which holds so much concern for each of us. And for assistance in the preparation of those pages, my greatest debt of gratitude is due Peter L. Ward, Chief, Branch of Earthquake Mechanics and Prediction, U.S. Geological Survey, who shared the enormous burden of gathering the latest research on seismic activity. I thank him for his professionalism and industry, and especially for his unbounded dedication and enthusiasm . . . a great sustaining force in itself.

Don DeNevi
Oakland, California

I

The
Inevitable
Disasters

For centuries the popular belief has been that America's earthquake hazards are limited to the Pacific coast. Such well-known disasters as the San Francisco earthquake in 1906, Long Beach in 1933, southern Alaska in 1964, and San Fernando in 1971, have contributed to this conception. In reality, however, all 50 states are subject to some earthquake-related hazard. Furthermore, 39 states containing nearly 53 percent of the population are in zones where moderate to major damage from earthquake shaking can occur.*

Although it's true that the most earthquake-prone areas in the United States are along the Pacific coast, much of the rest of the nation is susceptible to devastating seismic shocks. For example, Charleston, South Carolina, was heavily damaged in 1886. Also, highly destructive earthquakes occurred near New Madrid, Missouri, in 1811 and 1812 and were felt throughout the midwestern and the eastern United States. On several occasions, large earthquakes have struck the St. Lawrence River Valley, inflicting damage as far away as Boston.

---

*Wiggins, John H., et al, *Budgeting Justification for Earthquake Engineering Research*. Redondo Beach, CA: J. H. Wiggins Company (A report prepared for the National Science Foundation), 1974.

Considering the wide distribution of its large historic earthquakes, the United States has been remarkably fortunate in sustaining relatively few losses to date. The light losses (compared to earthquake losses in other parts of the world) have been due to Americans occupying vulnerable areas for a short time when compared to the recurrence interval of major seismic events, as well as because most large shocks have occurred during a time of day when casualties were relatively light. Also, by chance, local building materials and practices in the most seismically active parts of the nation produce structures which are traditionally more resistant to earthquakes than is construction in other parts of the United States—particularly compared to construction practices in those developing countries which have experienced major earthquake disasters.

U.S. earthquakes resulting in substantial property damage since 1865. The damage figures are in terms of the then-current dollar values and do not reflect inflation.

YEAR	LOCALITY	DAMAGE ($M)
1865	San Francisco, Calif.	.5
1868	San Francisco, Calif.	.4
1872	Owens Valley, Calif.	.3
1886	Charleston, S.C.	23.0
1892	Vacaville, Calif.	.2
1898	Mare Island, Calif.	1.4
1906	San Francisco, Calif.	24 .0
	Fire loss	500.0
1915	Imperial Valley, Calif.	.9
1918	Puerto Rico (tsunami damage from earthquake in Mona Passage)	4.0
1918	San Jacinto and Hemet, Calif.	.2
1925	Santa Barbara, Calif.	8.0
1933	Long Beach, Calif.	40.0

1935	Helena, Mont.	4.0
1940	Imperial Valley, Calif.	6.0
1941	Santa Barbara, Calif.	.1
1941	Torrance-Gardena, Calif.	1.0
1944	Cornwall, Canada-Massena, N.Y.	2.0
1946	Hawaii (tsunami damage from earthquake in Aleutians)	25.0
1949	Puget Sound, Wash.	25.0
1949	Terminal Island, Calif. (oil wells only)	9.0
1951	Terminal Island, Calif. (oil wells only)	3.0
1952	Kern County, Calif.	60.0
1954	Eureka-Arcata, Calif.	2.1
1954	Wilkes-Barre, Pa.	1.0
1955	Terminal Island, Calif. (oil wells only)	3.0
1955	Oakland-Walnut Creek, Calif.	1.0
1957	Hawaii (tsunami damage from earthquake in Aleutians)	3.0
1957	San Francisco, Calif.	1.0
1959	Hebgen Lake, Mont. (damage to timber and roads)	11.0
1960	Hawaii and U.S. West Coast (tsunami damage from earthquake off Chile coast)	25.5
1961	Terminal Island, Calif. (oil wells only)	4.5
1964	Alaska and U.S. West Coast (includes tsunami damage from earthquake near Anchorage)	500.0
1965	Puget Sound, Wash.	12.5
1966	Dulce, N. Mex.	.2
1969	Santa Rosa, Calif.	6.3
1971	San Fernando, Calif.	553.0
1973	Hawaii	5.6
1975	Aleutian Islands	3.5
1975	Idaho/Utah (Pocatello Valley)	1.0
1975	Hawaii	3.0
1975	Humboldt, Calif.	.3
1975	Oroville, Calif.	2.5
	Total	1878.0

*Deaths from U.S. earthquakes. Property damage
and loss of life are only two aspects of loss due to
earthquakes. Other losses include injuries, economic loss due to casualties, loss of income due
to business disruption, cost of emergency operations, etc. There is little available data on the extent of these indirect costs of earthquakes,
although they most certainly exceed the direct
costs.*

YEAR	LOCALITY	LIVES LOST
1811	New Madrid, Mo.	Several
1812	New Madrid, Mo.	Several
1812	San Juan Capistrano, Calif.	40
1868	Hayward, Calif.	30
1872	Owens Valley, Calif.	27
1886	Charleston, S.C.	60
1899	San Jacinto, Calif.	6
1906	San Francisco, Calif.	700
1915	Imperial Valley, Calif.	6
1918	Puerto Rico (tsunami from earth-quake in Mona Passage)	116
1925	Santa Barbara, Calif.	13
1926	Santa Barbara, Calif.	1
1932	Humboldt County, Calif.	1
1933	Long Beach, Calif.	115
1934	Kosmo, Utah	2
1935	Helena, Mont.	4
1940	Imperial Valley, Calif.	9
1946	Hawaii (tsunami from earthquake in Aleutians)	173
1949	Puget Sound, Wash.	8
1952	Kern County, Calif	14
1954	Eureka-Arcata, Calif.	1
1955	Oakland, Calif.	1
1958	Khantaak Island and Lituya Bay, Alaska	5

1959	Hebgen Lake, Mont.	28
1960	Hilo, Hawaii (tsunami from earth- quake off Chile coast)	61
1964	Prince William Sound, Alaska (tsunami)	131
1965	Puget Sound, Wash.	7
1971	San Fernando, Calif.	65
1975	Hawaii	2
	Total	1633

Tsunami-associated damage and loss of life in the U.S. Seismic seawaves, tsunamis, are often associated with large submarine or coastal zone earthquakes and can cause great damage by inundation and wave impact on shorelines thousands of miles from their source as well as on the shorelines near the epicenter of the earthquake which produces them. For example, Hilo, Hawaii, suffered extensive damage from a tsunami generated off the Chilean coast in 1960.

YEAR	DEAD	INJURED	ESTIMATED DAMAGE ($000)	AREA
1906	-	-	5	Hawaii
1917	-	-	*	American Samoa
1918	-	-	100	Hawaii
1918	40	-	250	Puerto Rico
1922	-	-	50	Hawaii California, American Samoa
1923	1	-	4,000	Hawaii
1933	-	-	200	Hawaii

Damage reported, but no estimates available

1946	173	163	25,000	Hawaii, Alaska, West Coast
1952	-	-	1,200	Midway Island, Hawaii
1958	2	-	50	Alaska
1957	-	-	4,000	Hawaii, West Coast
1960	61	282	25,500	Hawaii, West Coast, American Samoa
1964	122	200	104,000	Alaska, West Coast, Hawaii
1965	-	-	10	Alaska
1975	1	-	2,000	Hawaii

Earthquakes East of the Rockies

For too long, Americans have generally believed that the land east of the Rockies consisted of gently rolling hills and fertile plains, solid cities and benign towns, aging mountains and pastoral valleys, a gracefully quiet land compared with the rugged, young and often violent west. But scientists probing the earth's core and studying early eyewitness accounts of life across the United States are discovering that the eastern two-thirds is not so gentle, not so benign, nor so solid and secure. There are thousands of earthquake faults running deep below the eastern surface, with Manhattan Island located in the middle of a moderate earthquake zone. Each year millions of Americans feel the trembling of the eastern seaboard's 20 to 25 earthquakes.

The infrequency of the eastern earthquakes makes it necessary for scientists to disinter the past. Researching the archives as far back as 1550, they have been able to compile an earthquake profile for the east. More than 1,000 earthquakes have been reported east of the Mississippi River since 1700, particularly around Charleston, South Carolina; south of Cairo, Illinois; and north of the Adirondack mountains in upstate New York.

One of the most severe occurred in the winter of 1811–1812 when the entire Mississippi Valley was shaken violently in the region near the mouth of the Ohio River, 125 miles south of St. Louis. The small town of New Madrid, Missouri, appeared to be the hardest hit, and the shock could be felt as far away as Chicago, Washington, New Orleans and even 1,000 miles away in Quebec. It appears to have been a monster quake which makes the biggest known California earthquakes seem puny by comparison. Many states were devastated and whole forests fell for hundreds of miles all around. The course of the Mississippi River was changed. Entire islands disappeared. New lakes appeared all over the country, the biggest of which was Reelfoot Lake in Tennessee; dead tree stumps submerged in the lake are all that remain of the vast forests.

And, interestingly, history has virtually forgotten this great shake, probably because the midwest was sparsely populated in those days. It was the kind of disaster that people deliberately wanted to forget.

Apparently this, the greatest earthquake to ever hit the United States, shook the Mississippi and Ohio River valleys for weeks. However, three principal shocks were responsible for the greatest damage: (1) on December 16, 1811, at 2:00 A.M.; (2) on January 23, 1812; and (3) the largest on February 7, 1812 at 11:15 P.M. Devastation was everywhere in southeastern Mississippi, northeastern Arkansas, southwestern Kentucky and northwestern Tennessee. Hundreds of miles to the southeast of the epicenter, the earth apparently was uplifted 18 feet. What had been a lake along the St. Francis River simply vanished, leaving a sandy countryside littered with dead fish. Large fissures formed in the prairie. Eyewitnesses recorded they were so wide they could not be crossed

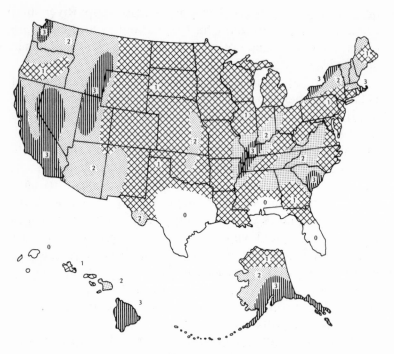

America's Earthquake Vulnerability. This ESSA/Coast and Geodetic Survey map indicates the degree of risk throughout the United States. Zone 0 can expect little or no damage; Zone 1 can expect minor damage (V and VI on the Mercalli scale); Zone 2 can expect moderate damage (VII on the Mercalli scale); Zone 3 can expect major damage (VIII and above on the Mercalli scale).

on horseback. Green farmland subsided to become swampland and numerous sandblows covered the ground with sand and mud.

Along a 75-mile stretch of the Mississippi in Tennessee, the river writhed like a snake. The banks fell in as the course of the river changed repeatedly. Great cracks opened and closed in the river bed, spouting waves of mud and water in the river. Ships capsized. No one ever knew how many people were killed or drowned in this calamity. Geologists and historians have speculated that the earthquake intensity covered about a million square miles. To illustrate how this earthquake makes the 1906 San Francisco earthquake seem like child's play, the equivalent intensity of shaking covered during the 1906 quake was only 56,000 square miles. If such a force as the 1812 earthquake hit Manhattan, it's obvious it would be the greatest disaster in American history.

On August 31, 1886, a lesser earthquake hit Charleston, South Carolina, which also rattled buildings in New York and as far west as St. Louis. Some 85 Charleston citizens were killed. Central Indiana was shaken the following year. In 1888, Charleston was hit again, and this time immense damage was done near the center of the city. Chimneys were toppled within a radius of 250 miles. Clocks were stopped nearly 700 miles away. Cities such as Chicago, Cleveland, New York, Boston, and others over a thousand miles away felt the shock in varying degrees. Most of these quakes were of Richter magnitude* between 3 and 5.

In contrast to the many active faults that scar California, not even the largest of the eastern earthquakes, particularly in the south, with the possible exception of the New

---

*The Richter magnitude scale, named after Dr. Charles F. Richter, Professor Emeritus of the California Institute of Technology, measures the energy of an eathquake at its source, and is the scale most commonly used, but most often misunderstood. On this scale, the earthquake's magnitude is expressed in whole numbers and decimals. However, Richter magnitudes can be confusing and misleading unless the mathematical basis for the scale is understood. It is important to recognize that magnitude varies logarithmically with the wave amplitude of the quake recorded by the seismograph. Each whole number step of magnitude on the scale represents an increase of 10 times in the measured wave amplitude of an earthquake, and an increase of 31 times in the amount of energy released by the quake. Thus, the amplitude of an 8.4 magnitude earthquake is not twice as large as a shock of magnitude 4.2, but 10,000 times as large. Correspondingly, a magnitude 8.4 earthquake releases almost one million times more energy than one of magnitude 4.2. A quake of magnitude 2 on the Richter scale is the smallest quake normally felt by humans.

Madrid quake, has produced any measurable displacement on known faults. This lack of observable movement may result from a deeper burial of the active seismic zones (which are harder to pinpoint) in the east as compared to California where the major fractures commonly intersect the surface. The lack of surface movement is probably also related to the generally lower energy level of eastern quakes. But as more and more geologists search the east, the more faulting they find.

Despite the lack of surface expression of active faults, most of the earthquakes recorded in the eastern United States during the past 200 years or more were concentrated along two main belts of seismic activity. A particularly young fault has been discovered in the coastal plains of Georgia. Although not clearly provable, some seismologists believe that its belt follows the Appalachian mountains from Georgia and western North Carolina to northern New England. It may be as young as 25,000 years old, which to geologists is a short time. The other belt includes the currently active New Madrid fault zone south of Cairo, Illinois, and stretches eastward, with some major gaps, to an equally active region northeast of the Adirondack mountains. This belt could be as young as a few thousand years or as old as 26 million. There has been no recently recorded earthquake activity around it. The question of its potency persists because historical records are lacking, and it is still not known whether or not its lines can soon produce earthquakes.

Seismograph data have been available only in the last 40 years, which is ample for the trembling west but not for the steadier east. The area in Missouri around the town of New Madrid, remains, as far as is known, the area of greatest energy release. The Charleston area remains the second major activity area where some 400 earthquakes have been recorded—three in 1976.

Three teams studying the Charleston area in the past few years have not found a specific fault and do not expect to find one, although recent satellite images suggest deeply buried fault lines cutting across the surface of the 13,000 square-mile area of the coastal plain from Washington, D.C., south to Charleston. Their results are not yet conclusive, but they deduce from high gravity and magnetic readings at the surface, from changes in deep stone, and from the concentrated tremor area that Charleston is different from other earthquake centers. Scientists emphasize that the faults do not present any known hazards.

In the west, it is at least scientifically comforting to be able to point to faults visible at the surface, measure the slippage, estimate the stress and perhaps predict or control future quakes. But the surface of the eastern United States shows no such overt signs. That placid surface conceals other nagging curiosities. Why is it that the shocks of Charleston and New Madrid made bricks shudder and flowers dance hundreds of miles away, while the great San Francisco earthquake, although apparently stronger, was not felt outside California?

Still, little has been spent to study eastern earthquakes, largely because few earthquakes in the east have been big enough to cause damage. When major earthquakes do occur, the interval between them is long. Unfortunately, with the scarcity of information on eastern quakes, scientists are farther away from understanding and making predictions on earthquakes in the east than are the geologists in the west. But now, the U.S. government is making some money available for earthquake research, mostly because of public concern over what could happen if an atomic power plant was struck by a tremor strong enough to initiate a nuclear disaster.

Scientists are hoping to learn when, where, and whether a large quake might indeed strike the eastern two-thirds of the country. Only now, with about $2 million provided by the Nuclear Regulatory Commission, is the U.S. Geological Survey able to install a network of 80 seismic stations in the northeast to test the earthquake danger to the proliferating nuclear power plants.

Dr. James Devine, the U.S. Geological Survey seismic expert, says, "The demands the public puts on safety limits on a nuclear plant are so severe that the estimates we made in the past are just not adequate. Up until a year or so ago there were only isolated incidents where we thought we could identify a fault that was generating earthquakes in the east. There is sufficient evidence to say that we're not going to have a Charleston-type earthquake up and down the coastal plain. Nor are we going to have a New Madrid-type of earthquake in downtown Chicago."

The only way to reach down and feel the fault zones is by drilling, and extensive drilling is very expensive and probably not productive, according to scientists.

As elsewhere, the laws of the universe fix the movements of the earth in the eastern part of the United States in their own space niche, but what of their place in the average American's perception?

In America's seismic zones about 100 million people live in houses, most of which have not been designed or engineered to resist earthquakes. It will certainly be many years before the principles and practices of earthquake-resistant buildings reach these areas. In the meantime, even in the cities, we shall have to continue for a long time yet to live and work in older buildings that are not earthquake-resistant, but which for a variety of reasons must remain in use.

It is this that makes it so important to develop the means to predict earthquakes. This will not prevent damage when an earthquake hits, but at least it will save lives if prediction can be made with the accuracy sufficient for public warning services.

The ultimate goal is to achieve immunity from America's earthquakes. Their occurrence is inevitable, although the disasters normally accompanying earthquakes need not be unavoidable. New techniques are being developed to minimize the disastrous effect.

Manhattan Cataclysm—A Scenario

> "And, behold . . . the earth did quake and the rocks rent . . ."
>
> St. Matthew's account of the first Good Friday.

There is something singularly shattering to the serenity of all human beings when the ground strains its thin coat and bursts its seams, spewing forth sudden destruction. Not appreciating that the earth is, after all, everyone's womb and tomb; people refuse to be troubled by the earthquake forecasts of scientists. So, when a major earthquake was predicted for Manhattan, even calamity-conditioned New Yorkers judged the news to be just so much fiction. No one dared to imagine what would happen if a major 8.3 Richter-sized earthquake hit the metropolis, especially during an evening rush hour. The possibility was presented to leading seismologists who offered the following scenario.

When the city and her 9 million citizens experienced a fearful repetition of that Good Friday earthquake over 2,000 years later, few people realized it would be one of the costliest catastrophies in the history of mankind. With its epicenter somewhere around the Pan American building on Park Avenue, and with a force ninety times stronger than the one that leveled Managua, Nicaragua, in 1972, thirty seconds seemed like an eternity as murderous destruction killed some 280,000 people.

It began years before that fatal Good Friday. Deep in the earth, perhaps as far down as 12 miles, fearful and little-understood forces were at work on the earth's crust, twisting and straining the great layers of rock as a truck strains its laminated springs going over a bump. Eventually, at a point called the focus, the rock gave way, snapping and shifting in an instant with the force of 12,000 Hiroshima-size atomic explosions. The devastation spread with terrible speed in an arc 500 miles long. Crackling through the earth at thousands of miles an hour, the shock wave sliced, churned, and ruptured the land like some enormous disk harrow drawn over the surface.

Striking during the peak of the 5:00 P.M. rush-hour stampede, the worst earthquake to ever hit the mid-Atlantic states struck without the warning shocks or minor tremors alerting homeward-bound commuters of possible disaster. The scenes witnessed during those agonizing, horrifying hours of aftershock, fire, and tidal waves were of staggering emotion. Jolting New Yorkers into instant terror, the entire cauldron of Manhattan Island rocked as the ground rippled and swelled. Accompanied by a roar which sounded like a thousand freight trains out of control, highways and avenues billowed with the upward thrust of the shock, buckling and pitching the thousands of cars and trucks that had been inching along the bridges over the railings. Buses, trains and ferries packed with helpless people were flung as if in a tornado. Great concrete slabs began overlapping one another like shingles set awry. Rail yards heaved and buckled, twisting tracks into bright curls of steel. With the downtown surfaces cracking open to release fiery blue arcs from electrical explosions and white plumes of water erupting from broken mains, many of the downtown skyscrapers, Manhattan's finest array of gleaming pinnacles of steel and glass, began to shudder and sway, loosening cascades of glass, ornamental stonework, and granite. Huge hunks of office buildings were shaken loose in tons in the first few seconds of violent vibration, zeroing in on screaming pedestrians. Shearing smaller luxury high-rises razor clean of penthouse patios, the people in their paths suffered horrible, bizarre deaths. Within those high-rises and office towers which had not collapsed, victims were flung across rooms. Windows and walls cracked and crumbled as the entire Manhattan skyline rocked like a huge clipper in a hurricane. Offices and apartments were a maelstrom of flying dishes, bookshelves, and wall hangings.

Four of Manhattan's six bridges and the four auto tunnels anchored in the underlying rock of the narrow rivers tumbled in like so many matchsticks and clay putty, plunging automobiles and pedestrians into the near-freezing waters. The remaining two bridges, the George Washington and Verranzano-Narrows, were whipping like giant snakes. The two great spans appeared to be holding, surviving the initial batterings. But their clogged approaches caved in, bringing down hundreds of cars with them. Landslides blocked the southern end of the George Washington bridge, trapping more helpless people. All four underwater links between Manhattan and the other boroughs tumbled in, drowning thousands of commuters in the terrifying darkness of the swaying tubes. Nearly all the subways were instantly buried by the sliding, groaning earth. Wall Street, the hub of the nation's financial life, became death row as older bank buildings came crashing down in masses of twisted steel and quivering debris. Among neat buildings and ordered streets, the earthquake seemed to give way to caprice, demolishing one building instantly and sparing its neighbor without so much as a broken window. Then, it would leap hundreds of yards, often as much as six blocks, to deliver massive, crushing jackhammer blows. Where high-tension power lines and fuel tanks lay, circuits ruptured; the crackle of their sparks was like the sputtering of fuses connected to gigantic powder magazines. When the power lines snapped, lights went off all over Manhattan, elevators stopped abruptly, trapping thousands of panicked office workers. Those on the ground floor of the famed Empire State building fled into the streets and were killed by the huge chunks of stone and concrete which came hurtling down from the aged structure. Strangely, all the occupants of the 102 story building survived without serious wounds. But others in the world's densest concentration of businessmen and secretaries, of salesmen and psychiatrists, were not so lucky. Even with the most sound construction, collapsing ceilings, tunnels, and concrete overpasses took their death toll. Only 30 seconds had elapsed since the first jolt was felt, but everywhere there was unbelievable agony and destruction.

While the shock waves were racing along the length of Manhattan, blazing gas mains were already setting off fires in the quake's wake. Fires began erupting everywhere, ignited by short circuits and fed by the leaking gas mains. One had instantly touched the gigantic reading room of the New York Public Library at Fifth Avenue and 42nd Street. Fire fighters had quickly scrambled into action, but their trucks could not negotiate torn-up streets. Because of broken water mains, fire hydrants were useless. All the city's phones were dead and the few rescuers already at work were further hampered by the destruction of medical supplies—including crucial blood plasma—and the collapse of nearly all Manhattan's hospitals.

The United Nations Secretariat building occupying six blocks on the East Side collapsed in a shower of glass, cutting and mangling thousands of office workers leaving the building on their way home. The upheaval tossed chunks of the street in front of the UN around like children's blocks, squashing cars and trucks.

In lower Manhattan, the two 110-story towers of the World Trade Center simply tumbled down into the Hudson River, a sight too incredible to believe.

Dust and smoke-blinded pedestrians who survived the initial shock, milled about the toppled buildings and brick-piled avenues in stunned horror. Many began struggling down to Battery Park, a small open area where they thought they might be safe from falling glass and masonry. In their paths, however, were raised barriers of jagged pieces of roadway up to 15 feet high. Immense human traffic jams developed as people fought each other to scramble out of the traps. But the second and third tremors to hit once culturally rich Manhattan a few minutes later opened further huge cracks in the earth which also began swallowing up buildings and terrified people. Manhattan appeared to be a bombed-out city.

In the wake of the three shocks, the Hudson and East Rivers rushed out of the tidal basin exposing long-lost sunken ships and schools of flapping fish, and retreated down the Narrows of the bay to the Atlantic. People caught on the beach of Coney Island found the sand disappearing under their feet. Somewhere off New York's southern coast, the sea bottom had heaved and plunged violently, setting millions of tons of water in motion, first in retreat and then forward as a monstrous battering ram. The water rushed back up the Narrows in a 100-foot-high wave which nearly toppled the Statue of Liberty. Crashing over the Manhattan docks and rolling over the screaming survivors, it swept everything in its path, flooding and drowning helpless people in subways and basements all the way up to Rockefeller Center. Death and destruction lay everywhere, capriciously characterized by corpses dotting the sickening jumble of twisted steel.

In those agonizing moments, New York City suffered more than $750,000,000,000 worth of property damage, to say nothing of an awesome toll in life. It was not even the ultimate earthquake that scientists had long predicted for the eastern seaboard.

* * *

Have you been sitting in your local theater watching a multimillion dollar soap opera unfold? Are you watching a quake created by "Sensurround," a system hooked under your seat and into the film's soundtrack which is setting off a high-level tremor at the cost of $500 per week to the theater's owner in order to give you a $3.50 artistic disaster thrill?

Although this script might be added to the growing list*

---

*Added to this list was the recent announcement by Warner Brothers Studios in Burbank that shooting would soon begin on a new film entitled "Cracking-Up." The story is about an earthquake fault which splits southern California, leaving behind an indestructible inquiring tv reporter who searches out survivors in order to learn what they were doing when the quake hit!

The distribution of populations by risk zones

RISK ZONE	POPULATION		NUMBER OF STATES AFFECTED
	MILLIONS	% of TOTAL	
0 (low)	17	8	5
1	115	57	42*
2	40	20	39
3 (high)	31	15	21
TOTAL	203		51*

*Including the District of Columbia.

of movies like "Towering Inferno," "Tidal Wave," and "Earthquake" which have mesmerized audiences of disaster buffs over the past few years, earthquake terror is taking on an entirely new meaning across the entire American continent. Few locations are immune from the catastrophe, calamity, and cataclysm of a shifting and shuddering earth. Although tremors actually strike the Pacific west coast ten times more than the Atlantic east coast, such widely dispersed cities as Boston and Charleston, Memphis and Buffalo are vulnerable to strong seismic shocks. With the Ramapo Fault* crossing the Hudson river above Manhattan at the Tappan Zee bridge near the Indian Rock nuclear power plant, it is entirely conceivable that the most famous city in the world could be toppled by one of nature's greatest disasters.

The potential Manhattan earthquake is presumptuous, though possible. More probable is the earthquake danger ever-present in California.

---

*Faults are fractures or fracture zones in the earth along which there has been movement of the rocks on either side. The total movement that has taken place over many thousands of years may be a few inches or many miles. Most earthquakes result from the sudden rupture of rocks.

II

Learning to Live with California's Recurring Earthquakes

Although the earth never rests in fault-ridden California, damaging earthquakes in her urban regions have been relatively rare compared with the tornadoes, hurricanes, floods, blizzards and other disasters that annually afflict substantial populations elsewhere. Indeed, Californians have become relaxed about the potential for death. A recent Mervin Field poll indicated that 40 percent of the state's population thought it was "quite unlikely" they would someday be affected by earthquakes. Only 20 percent said they were worried. When people were asked what they would do if their government predicted a major quake, only 25 percent said they would move out of the area temporarily and only 12 percent said they would move away permanently. In other words, 88 percent of the population would stay and ride out an earthquake, even if a big one were predicted.

Yet, the low frequency of strong earthquakes must be weighed against their high death-dealing and destructive potential. Possible fatalities from a single major earthquake have been estimated at up to 10,000 for the San Francisco Bay area, and up to 20,000 in the Los Angeles area (excluding estimates of life loss caused by dam failure). As many as 40,000 in the San Francisco Bay area and 80,000 in the Los Angeles area might suffer severe injuries. Estimates of possible property damage range between $5 billion and $50 billion in a single major quake affecting a large urban region.

The combination of relatively low odds with such potentially disastrous consequences makes the earthquake hazard difficult to cope with. The smaller, more recent quakes have not centered on heavily populated areas. Since 1812, a total of 26 damaging earthquakes have struck California, inflicting a total life loss of 1,020 and dollar property losses in excess of $1 billion in dollar values at the time of the earthquake, or more than $7 billion in 1971 dollar value.

Accordingly, Californians must be considered lucky in terms of the recent history of major seismic events. The biggest quakes took place in the 1800s, and since 1906, the state has not experienced an earthquake equal to the one that ravaged San Francisco.

Meanwhile, the state has grown, placing increasingly larger populations at risk. Moreover, we know that future destructive earthquakes are inevitable. Sooner or later major quakes will strike one or more urbanized regions, with possibly devastating consequences unless effective measures are taken to reduce the risks.

For example, scientists are certain that a major earthquake will occur in the San Francisco Bay area. The only question is when will it strike? A glance at the comparatively brief historic record of this region shows that five destructive earthquakes have struck the area in the two centuries which comprise its historic records. The great 1906 San Francisco earthquake had surface faulting (fractures in the earth's crust) which extended for over 400 kilometers, parting as much as 7 meters.

Today, the urban area in America most likely to experience severe destruction during a large earthquake is San Francisco's Chinatown. The crowded, densely populated district contains hundreds of unreinforced, unsafe brick buildings, and their facades are studded with unstable parapets

Losses Due to Earthquake Shaking in California.*

Date	Location	Lives Lost	Dollar Loss ** at the Time of the Quake
1812---	San Juan Capistrano ...	40	--
1857---	Fort Tejon	--	--
1865---	San Francisco.	--	500,000
1868---	Hayward.	30	350,000
1872---	Owens Valley	27	250,000
1892---	Vacaville	--	225,000
1898---	Mare Island	--	1,400,000
1899---	San Jacinto	6	--
1906---	San Francisco.	700	500,000,000
1915---	Imperial Valley	6	900,000
1918---	San Jacinto and Hemet .	--	200,000
1925---	Santa Barbara	13	8,000,000
1933---	Long Beach	115	40,000,000
1940---	Imperial Valley	9	6,000,000
1941---	Santa Barbara	--	100,000
1941---	Torrance-Gardena.	--	1,100,000
1949---	Terminal Island	--	9,000,000
1951---	Terminal Island	--	3,000,000
1952---	Kern County	14	60,000,000
1954---	Eureka-Arcata	1	2,000,000
1955---	Terminal Island	--	3,000, 000
1955---	Oakland-Walnut Creek. .	1	1,000,000
1957---	San Francisco.	--	1,000,000
1961---	Terminal Island	--	4,500,000
1969---	Santa Rosa	--	8,350,000
1971---	San Fernando	58	504,950,000
	Totals	1,020	$1,155,825,000

*After Coffman (1969) and the Los Angeles County Earthquake Commission (1971.).

**Figures reflect losses due to property damage and do not include other socio-economic costs. If converted to 1971 dollars, the total loss would be $7,200,000,000 (Mukerjee, unpublished).

which represent a major collapse hazard. As seismologists have long been declaring publicly, another great earthquake in California is inevitable. Robert M. Hamilton, chief of the Office of Earthquake Studies for the U.S. Geological Survey in Reston, Virginia, adds "The further in time you are from the last great quake, the closer you are to the next one."

Because the stresses on California's San Andreas fault are steadily building up, the great rift is bound to slip with an enormous jolt somewhere along its 650 mile length sooner or later. Hamilton argues, "Californians should not ignore or underestimate the earthquake threat. Nor should irrational fear of earthquakes be a diversion from rational preparations. But preparation for a quake poses difficult political, social, and economic problems, and Chinatown's danger typifies them. The area abounds with unreinforced parapets certain to rain bricks on the narrow and potentially crowded streets below in a significant earthquake. Most of the buildings are constructed of unreinforced masonry walls with many weakening openings. The engineers are certain that many of these buildings will collapse in an earthquake like the one that struck in 1906, burying the occupants in mounds of rubble no less tragically than in Guatemala, China, or Turkey this past year."

California's major earthquakes have occurred on two well-known geologically active faults. The greater of these two faults, the San Andreas, goes through the San Francisco area and runs very close to Los Angeles. It has often been termed California's "master fault."

Geologic studies show that many major earthquakes have occurred on this fault over the past millions of years, and there is no reason to believe that earthquakes on it will suddenly cease now. A major line of evidence is the fact that parts of the San Andreas fault are slowly "creeping." Creeping means that the land masses on one side of the fault are moving with respect to the other side, but moving so slowly that only instruments can record these displacements.

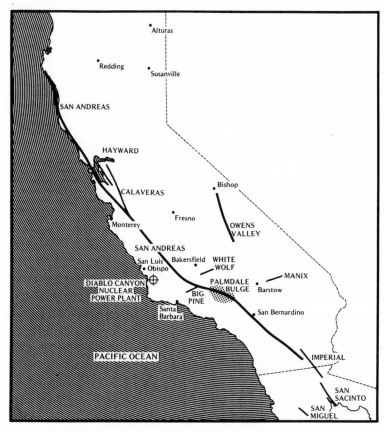

California's Active Faults.

This creep is not associated with recorded earthquakes, but is an evidence of strains within the earth's crust. The most prominent example is a winery south of San Francisco on the San Andreas fault which has been in the process of being torn apart at the rate of over 1 centimeter per year for at least the past 50 years.

So, the 100 million-year-old San Andreas fault is a fracture in the earth's crust along which two parts of the crust have slipped with respect to each other. It is the master fault of an intricate network of faults that cuts through the rocks of the coastal region of California. It extends some 600 miles and is as deep as 20 miles in the earth's crust. In detail it is a complex zone of crushed and broken rock from a few hundred feet to a mile wide. If one were to fly over the area, one would see the stark crack across the arid plain north of Los Angeles where the San Andreas fault marks a boundary where the two slabs of the earth's crust rub together. Pulverized rock, the debris of milenniums of grinding, clog the clefts. When these segments slip, earthquakes wrack the land; one slip of up to 21 feet, for example, gutted San Francisco in 1906.

On the other hand, there exists the potentially more dangerous Hayward fault which goes through major population areas within the suburbs of San Francisco. The Hayward fault has had major earthquakes, and fault creep is taking place on it. It is easy to conclude, therefore, that a major earthquake is a reasonable probability in the foreseeable future. It is understandable why scientists are using this area as one of the several testing grounds for earthquake prediction research.

As we know, earthquakes in themselves are not a significant hazard. The documented cases of a fault opening up and encompassing people and then burying them can perhaps be counted on one's fingers. Landslides can and do take a very significant toll of lives, but in most cases these hazards are relatively self-evident before the earthquake and do not need an earthquake to trigger them. The major life hazard in the usual earthquake is from the collapse of man-made structures such as buildings and dams. This is certainly true for San Francisco as well as for all of California.

One of the more interesting studies of California's fault lines can be found in Cienega Valley, south of Hollister in the central coast range. This area is a peaceful vale far from major roads and urban sprawl. Grass and live oaks cover the low hills on either side, and the valley floor and lower slopes are planted in grapes. This has long been a good producing valley for the Almaden wine district. Sheds and buildings belonging to a modest winery have stood beside the Cienega Road for many decades. The San Francisco earthquake and resulting fire of 1906 brought members of at least one new family to the valley. After losing their city home in that disaster they settled down to the peaceful, quiet life of vintner. They built a new house—right over the San Andreas fault.

Cienega is laced with faults. For this reason, Cienega Valley has become the most studied segment of the San Andreas fault. The reason for the popularity of this locale is the winery. One of the original buildings fell down in 1939 and was replaced by a stronger one with massive concrete floors and walls. Once again, the employees of the winery found that part of their job consisted of patching cracks in the floor and walls and shoring up studs that kept slipping off their foundations. In 1956 scientists discovered what the owners had known for a long time. The winery building was slowly being wrenched apart by the San Andreas fault, which passes right under the main building. There are other signs of slippage; the offset rows of grapevines just south of the building and the repeated breaking of the concrete walls of a nearby drainage channel. Since 1956 geophysicists have been carefully measuring the displacements, and much of our knowledge of the mechanics of creep along a fault zone comes from this study.

We know that the Pacific Plate is moving an average of two inches per year to the northwest. Scientists have arrived at this rate by direct measurements in recent years along the San Andreas fault, by a study of magnetic strips embedded in the oceanic crust and by comparing the offset of rock formations of various ages along the San Andreas. This movement has been going on for millions of years and certainly is not about to stop.

Indeed, the Farallones, the craggy islands beyond the Golden Gate Bridge, are sailing toward Alaska a centimeter or two a year. They've been headed that direction for eons. The movement, of course, confirms that just to their east, the earth's crust is bending under the growing strain along the San Andreas fault. Laser measurements from Mt. Diablo's tip to the Farallones indicate that the islands have traveled five feet to the north since the 1906 earthquake. Indeed, that shock shoved San Francisco 10 feet closer to Los Angeles.

It is also interesting to note that the west side of the San Andreas fault with Los Angeles sitting on top of it is grinding northward at the rate of about 2 inches a year. Thus, descendants living in San Francisco ten million years from now will be able to reach Los Angeles merely by walking to the west side of Daly City—by then Los Angeles will have become a new suburb of the Bay area. This is based on recent discoveries that the San Andreas is one of many, jagged rifts in the earth which separate the huge tectonic plates of moving crust. Los Angeles sits on the northward-moving Pacific Plate, while San Francisco stands on the western edge of the more stable North American Plate. Robert Hamilton of the U.S. Geological Survey laughs: "For those who feel that San Francisco possesses a certain charm and unique lifestyle incompatible with that of Los Angeles, the unwelcome rafting of the southern metropolis to this area would seem to call for an environmental impact statement. But although an environmental impact statement can delay or stop most undertakings in this day and age, there is little hope it could interfere with the earth's restless movement. The consolation is that in 60 million years, Los Angeles will have passed San Francisco by and will have moved to the coast of southern Alaska. There Los Angeles will be carried down into the interior of the earth to be melted down and recycled, reappearing on the earth's surface in the far distant future during a volcanic eruption."

Wobbling Los Angeles

To scientists, the most disturbing thing about the 1971 San Fernando earthquake was that it was almost certainly not the great quake that scientists and soothsayers have been forecasting for years. The odds are high that sometime in the not too distant future somewhere along the California coast the same thing is going to happen again, but this time only worse.

For California, as we know, is riven by one of the longest, most dangerous geological fractures in the earth's crust—the San Andreas fault, the 600-mile long dislocation that courses inland from the Gulf of California into the Mexican state of Baja California, running up through San Bernardino 35 miles east of Los Angeles, passing through San Francisco and moving out to sea again near Mendocino in the northern part of the state. What shocked scientists was that the San Fernando quake struck in an area that had been seismically inactive at least since the end of the last Ice Age—about 10,000 years ago.

California is perched on the so-called "Ring of Fire," an earthquake and volcano-prone region that circles the Pacific basin. It reaches as far south as New Zealand on the west, north through Japan, across the Aleutians and down the coast of the Americas on the east. Only recently have geophysicists begun to understand what stokes the ring's "fires"—the tectonic plates. But strangely enough, the San Fernando quake did not occur along the San Andreas fault or any of the active faults that are associated with it. It originated some distance away, along a swath roughly 20-miles long, running at approximately right angles to the big fault. It is in this area that the San Gabriel mountains, north of Los Angeles, meet the San Fernando valley. Judging by ruptures in this surface and readings from their instruments, scientists concluded that the mountains had either pushed a few feet over the valley, or that the valley had thrust underneath the mountains. However it occurred, the sudden, complex movements led to a significant quake—strong enough to tumble walls and knock down highway bridges.

Some scientists speculated that the gravitational forces exerted by the direct alignment of the sun, moon, and earth during that period's lunar eclipse may have been sufficiently strong to trigger the release of the forces slowly stored up in a long inactive fault zone. Others thought that the quake might be connected with the slight eccentric movements of the spinning earth known as "Chandler's Wobble." Such wobbling can displace the earth's axis of rotation at the poles by as much as 70 feet during a year. In addition, there is a seven-year cycle of daily motion, which reached a peak during 1971. Some scientists have suggested that increases in earthquakes can be expected as a result of an increase in the amount of wobble. Other scientists are skeptical. They argue that they don't know if quakes cause the wobble or the wobble causes the quakes.

But there is one thing scientists agree on: the slow, steady buildup of strain that has long been taking place along the San Andreas fault was not released by the quake. In fact, land on opposite sides of the fault remained ominously still during the tremors. Some scientists feel that the stress along the fault may even have been increased. In any case, most scientists are convinced that the stored-up energy must eventually be freed. This most certainly could cause a far more powerful quake which could kill tens of thousands of helpless human beings. When? No one knows.

The Los Angeles Predicament

During the last two centuries of recorded history in southern California there have been three major temblors: the 1872 Owens Valley earthquake, the 1857 Ft. Tejon earthquake, and an 1892 earthquake in Baja. As far as can be determined

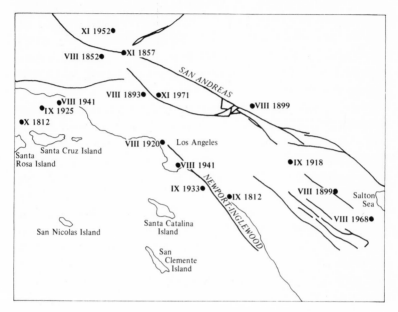

Earthquakes in the Los Angeles Area. Locations of major historical earthquakes recorded as VIII or above on the Mercalli scale.

all three shocks had a magnitude greater than 8 on the Richter scale. The two closest to present-day Los Angeles were the 1812 and 1857 earthquakes. The 1857 quake occurred on the San Andreas fault and surface rupture is believed to have extended southward toward San Bernardino, and been as long as 275 miles. The exact location of the actual epicenter is unimportant since faulting extended over the portion of the San Andreas fault closest to Los Angeles, as determined by damage in the area. At its nearest point, the San Andreas fault is about 38 miles from the center of downtown Los Angeles. Thus, more than 100 years ago, a huge earthquake with associated fault rupture occurred on the San Andreas along the portion of the fault closest to Los Angeles. A section of the fault rupture and the consequent radiation of seismic waves were within 35–40 miles of the city center. By comparison, the 1906 San Francisco earthquake happened on a segment of the San Andreas fault which at its closest point was about 7 miles from downtown. The location of the epicenter of the 1812 earthquake in the Santa Barbara Channel was perhaps 75 miles from the heart of Los Angeles.

The most damaging earthquake to strike the Los Angeles-Orange County area was the famed March 10, 1933, Long Beach temblor which occurred on the Newport-Inglewood fault. With a foreshock of magnitude 4 taking place on the preceding day, the epicenter of the main shock was located about two miles offshore southwest of Huntington Beach. This earthquake was a major calamity for the Los Angeles area, particularly in the nearby cities of Long Beach, Compton, Torrance, and Garden Grove, where 120 people were killed.

But the California earthquake most analyzed for possible repetition is the 1971 San Fernando earthquake. Data on loss of life, injuries, and property damage are more available for this tragedy than for any other American earthquake. Although the magnitude was only 6.6, the approximate length of surface faulting was 12 miles, resulting in 58 deaths and over 5,000 injured. Occurring at 6:01 A.M., most of the area's 7 million people were in their wood-frame homes. The collapses at the Veterans Hospital in the foothills of the San Fernando Valley immediately claimed 47 lives. An additional nine deaths were due to heart attacks from the psychological impact of the earthquake.

Recently, a possible precursor of a great earthquake in southern California was discovered. Robert Hamilton, chief of the U.S. Geological Survey's office of Earthquake Studies in the Department of Interior in Washington, D.C., told a press conference that a section of Pasadena had dropped five to six inches in the past few years. Using delicate instruments which can accurately measure changes of more than 1/1,000 of a foot in elevation in relation to sea level, Hamilton said the Pasadena subsidence may be part of the same land deformation which produces the famed 60-mile-wide Palmdale Bulge, an area along the San Andreas fault northeast of Los Angeles which has risen dramatically since 1959. Recently, parts of that perplexing and ominous bulge, a hugh oval section which rose about 12 inches above the surrounding countryside during the 1960s, seemed to be falling also. In Japan and the United States, such abrupt deformations have preceded some devastating quakes. Hamilton, however, cautioned that it is not yet possible to predict the exact time, place, and magnitude of a coming quake and added that such deformations may occur without temblors taking place.

Most seismologists feel that southern California will be hit sooner than the equally active area of northern California by a devastating earthquake and that shock will be severe. Said Hamilton, "Every passing day brings the disaster closer. I feel the decrease by seven inches of the ground swelling near Palmdale, a desert town about 65 miles north of Los Angeles, during the last three years is quite mystifying. Californians should not ignore or underestimate the earthquake threat, nor should irrational fears be allowed to be a diversion from rational preparations. Massive stresses are accumulating along the San Andreas fault. When they snap, a major earthquake will occur."

To provide essential data for effective predisaster planning for major damaging earthquakes which could affect the Los Angeles metropolitan area, the Federal Disaster Assistance Administration estimated deaths and damages to facilities particularly critical to disaster relief and recovery. The administration's problem was to determine what might occur if a shock with the magnitude of 8.3 on the Richter scale hit the city at 2:30 A.M., 2:00 P.M., and 4:30 P.M. Casualty estimates were determined by population distributions in various types of dwellings.

As far as night time casualties were concerned, the investigators projected a reasonable death ratio of 12 deaths per 100,000, or about that experienced in the 1971 San Fernando earthquake. Such a death ratio is based on the fact that the population is essentially indoors in relatively safe wooden dwellings at 2:30 A.M. and that 12 deaths per 100,000 was that experienced in the 6:00 A.M. 1971 San Fernando earthquake. This death ratio would of course decrease with distance from the causative fault. Construction units more than one story in height are not as safe as wood-frame buildings and the death ratio would be higher. Also, high-rise buildings at large distances from the epicenter are more likely to suffer major damage than are low structures.

Earthquake deaths and injuries vary considerably depending upon the location of the epicenter, the magnitude of the earthquake, the time of day, and the ability of the buildings in the impact area to withstand the shock. Of course, in addition to the direct losses measured by property damage, death, and injury, an earthquake results in many indirect losses due to disruption of the community and anguish suffered by people. Survivors of the 1977 earthquake in Bucharest, Romania, described the psychological impact of the quake as worse than that experienced in World War II. Many children who were in the 1971 San Fernando earthquake required analysis and counseling for neuroses caused by the event.

Predicting deaths is more complicated and less subject to reliable analysis for daytime earthquakes than for those occurring at night. Many of the 9 million people in the metropolitan area of Los Angeles will be at work in structures not as safe as their wood-frame residences. At 2:00 P.M., others will be at home, or in small shopping areas, schools, small industrial plants, or in office buildings of various sizes. Some will be on the streets in more hazardous areas. Streets during the middle of the afternoon will not be as crowded as during the commute hours. As one basis for analysis, the investigators used the death ratio of nine killed for every 100,000 in the 1964 Anchorage, Alaska, earthquake which occurred late in the day on Good Friday.

	RESULTANT DEATHS		
PROJECTED EARTHQUAKES	2:30 A.M.	2:00 P.M.	4:30 P.M.
San Andreas fault with magnitude of 8.3 on Richter Scale:	2,790	11,259	12,385
Newport-Inglewood fault, with magnitude of 7.5 on Richter Scale:	4,090	18,843	20,728

As far as deaths occurring at 4:30 P.M., the ratio may be seven killed for every 100,000 because many people who were in offices and in other places of employment would now be on the streets. One mitigating factor in overall casualties is the fact that schools are generally closed by 4:30 P.M.

"Los Angeles will undoubtedly suffer a maximum 8.5 magnitude earthquake soon," says Dr. Charles Richter, inventor of the quake-magnitude scale. "But a quake involving the entire San Andreas fault which runs from north of San Francisco to the bottom of California, or the Newport-Inglewood fault which runs through downtown Los Angeles, seems incredible to believe. Although a future quake is not likely to be much more powerful than the 1857 Ft. Tejon quake rated at 8.3, it really was the last major southern California jolt. A figure of 200 years is the average length of time between major quakes in southern California. That means that the next one could be as little as 60 years away or as long as 400 years away."

Today, the main thrust by the federal, state and local governments, as well as concerned private organizations, is towards the vital human needs which are required immediately after the disaster. With substantially less attention paid to long-range effects, the groups have identified three major concerns:

1. Effects on local medical resources,
2. Demands on medical resources,
3. Effects on immediate and vital public needs.

Emphasis is placed on the earthquake effects on local hospitals and also on some aspects of the post-disaster status of local medical personnel and local medical supplies. For example, it is projected that during the first few hours, the large majority of people in the affected downtown Los Angeles areas will not have vital immediate needs other than the basic requirements of adequate food, shelter, and water supplies. Actually, the need for an adequate supply of water for human consumption, plus that needed for fire fighting, is probably more vital than shelter or food in the first day or two that follow, since the Los Angeles climate tends to be moderate and also since a minimal food supply exists in homes. Obviously, such an immediate need for water cannot be met in terms of hours if the water system is out of service. The large number of earthquake resistive structures found in the public school systems and the recently constructed shopping centers would be a major resource for temporary housing and feeding. Local stocks of non-refrigerated foods will last for days and in the residential sections the stocks will last several days, also. But the major problem exists in the distribution of foods arriving from outside sources if main transportation arteries are closed. Needless to say, a rapid restoration of communications, transportation facilities, and public utilities is vital.

No one need speculate the cost to property damage if an 8.3 earthquake hit Los Angeles. Nor does one need to weigh what such a shock would do in terms of the economy: the temporary loss of jobs as a result of damage to factories, the temporary loss of transport and supply lines to and from these places of employment, and other economic dislocations. Also, Pacific Ocean pollution problems from oil spills, emergency chemical discharges, and raw sewage discharge due to damaged treatment plants would be immense.

Unanticipated events happen in almost every earthquake. In downtown Los Angeles, a destructive shock may occur on an unexpected fault as it did in the 1971 San Fernando shock, although this is not considered likely for a huge earthquake. And, the temblor could occur during the height of the Christmas shopping season. In Los Angeles, the earthquake could occur on one of those days each year when the thick ground fog stops all air transportation for hundreds of miles around, thereby restricting aid via the air.

No one will ever be able to predict accurately the number of dead and injured resulting from an 8.3 shock to Los Angeles. To evaluate this kind of intensity critically, seismologists must take into account the duration of shaking (over 30 seconds can reduce even the strongest structures to rubble), the nature of the ground underneath the locality, whether the surface is level, gently sloping or steep, whether people were indoors or outdoors, in what kind of structure, on what floor, whether quiet or active, and if active how occupied. Also, the seismologists must analyze whether the motion is rapid or slow, simple or complex, and whether it begins gradually or abruptly. These and numerous other considerations must be analyzed before predicting human and structural losses. But one thing is certain among seismologists: the Palmdale Bulge has dropped seven inches during the past three years, suggesting that massive stresses are accumulating in the ground which one day must be unleashed. When that happens, Los Angeles may suffer the worst earthquake in her history.

* * *

Some scientists feel that it is possible that the next big shaking in southern California could set off shocks in faults adjacent to the San Andreas. If that should occur 375 miles to the north in San Francisco, the result would be disastrous.

In recognition of such a need for effective predisaster planning for a possible 8.3 earthquake catastrophe, the Office of Emergency Preparedness entered into an agreement with the Earth Sciences Laboratories of the National Oceanic and Atmospheric Administration to determine the loss of life and damage to San Francisco. Special emphasis was devoted to estimating damage to those facilities particularly critical to disaster relief and recovery.

During the past 140 years, the San Francisco Bay area has suffered a number of severe earthquakes. Of these, the earliest large shock known occurred in June of 1836 along the Hayward fault in the East Bay and may have had a magnitude of 8.3. The next severe shock in late June 1838, occurred on the San Andreas fault in the foothills west of Palo Alto. This temblor has also been compared in magnitude with the famed shock of April 18, 1906. At the time, the San Francisco business district was called Yerba Buena. It consisted of not more than eight or ten simple wooden structures and the immediate area had no more than 60 or 70 people.

But by 1865, five- and six-story buildings had been built in San Francisco, a booming city of over 150,000. On October 9 of that year, an earthquake occurred which the *Alta California* described as "violent." The front page observed, "Well-built structures on good ground survived the shaking effects of earthquakes better than structures on made-ground. It is a noticeable fact that not one building having walls properly secured and laid in cement, with sound foundations, suffered by the earthquake in the least."

Again, the estimated intensity is 8.3, with the epicentral region somewhere in the hills south of San Francisco, probably in the Santa Cruz Mountains.

Three years later, the young metropolis was rocked again by a severe earthquake which incurred the first loss of life. With 12 people killed and over $400,000 property damage to the structures built on "made-ground" and mud-flats all around the Bay, the shock is estimated to have had a magnitude of 7.5.

The most significant earthquake in the history of the Bay area in terms of lives lost and property damage was the earthquake of April 18, 1906. Surface faulting was observed nearly 270 miles in length from Point Arena in the north, all the way south to Hollister. Incredible displacements of up to

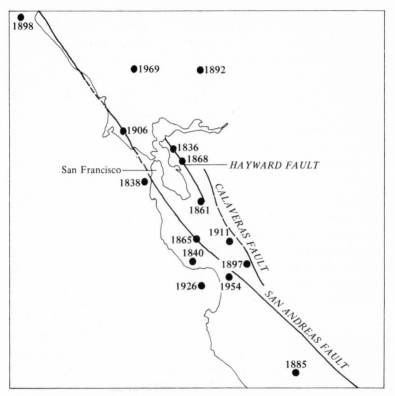

Earthquakes in the San Francisco Bay Area. Locations of major historical earthquakes recorded as VIII or above on the Mercalli scale.

25 feet were recorded in the San Andreas rift zone north of San Francisco. This temblor was felt as far away as 400 miles in such towns and cities as Coos Bay in Oregon, Winnemucca in Nevada, and Los Angeles. The sudden shock severed water mains in San Francisco, Santa Rosa, and Fort Ross, depriving fire-fighing units of their necessary water supply. Over 700 lives were lost during the earthquake and fire which followed. $400 million worth of property was destroyed.

Although many other earthquakes have occurred in the

Bay area since then, none have been very damaging. On March 22, 1957, an earthquake with a magnitude of 5.3 occurred just south of San Francisco which damaged frame houses west of Daly City.

During the past 20 years, the largest earthquakes to have occurred in the Bay area had magnitudes of 5.6 and 5.7 in and around the city of Santa Rosa, a large city 50 miles north of San Francisco.

However, moderate earthquake activity takes place every day along portions of the San Andreas, Hayward, and Calaveras fault zones which pass under the Bay area. It has been noted that small episodic earth movements are also taking place along these active faults at a rate of a few centimeters each year.

Expected deaths and injuries resulting from earthquakes in the Bay area will be principally due to the failures of man-made facilities, such as buildings and doors. While earthquake-induced landslides may cause loss of life during the wet season, there is no possibility of the type of landslide which led to 25,000 to 30,000 deaths after the 1970 Peruvian earthquake.* Tsunamis (seismic sea waves) have always been a negligible threat in the Bay area. In contrast, 92 percent of all the deaths in the 1964 Alaskan earthquake were attributed to the sea waves.

From previous earthquake experiences, it can be assumed that during night hours, an 8.3 magnitude shock on either the Hayward or San Andreas fault will result in 12 deaths per 100,000 people in wood-framed structures. This ratio is the same as that of the area experiencing the heaviest shaking in the 1971 San Fernando shock. Applying this ratio to *all* of the area will lead to results which are on the high side, but probably not unduly so. For one reason, more older structures exist in the intensity regions than in the small area

---

*Yet it is possible that several hundred lives will be lost when ocean-fronting bluffs in Daly City, California slide into the Pacific Ocean after a major shock.

of highest intensity in San Fernando, resulting in heavier casualties. Also, the high population concentrations are close to the two faults. And, San Francisco and Daly City have a specialized type of two-story wood-frame dwelling in which the front of the first story often has excessive openings and the first story also has few interior partitions. As a result, the first story of this type of dwelling is much weaker than the average of those in the San Fernando sample area.

The rest of the population which is not in wood-frame structures at night will be in buildings of a higher hazard. Using various technical considerations for the remaining 1,200,000 downtown area inhabitants, a total of 2,300 deaths would occur for a magnitude 8.3 earthquake on either the San Andreas or the Hayward fault, a death ratio of 50/100,000.

Possible deaths occurring at 2:00 P.M. is far more complicated to predict. Most of the 4,600,000 people in the area will be at work in structures which are not as safe as their wood-frame residences. Other people will either be at home, in small shopping areas, safe schools, moderately safe industrial plants, and office buildings of various quality. Although some people will be in the streets, those streets will not be as clogged as during the commuting hours.

If an earthquake with a magnitude of 8.3 hit at 4:30 P.M., deaths are estimated to be about the same as the 2:00 P.M. hour, except that 600,000 or more people will be heading home. Thus, an increase can be expected due to a large number of deaths and injuries on the freeways as well as people being crushed under falling objects from buildings. The National Oceanic and Atmospheric Administration projects the total number of San Francisco deaths at 4:30 P.M. as:

6,040 deaths
   400 (additional freeway killed)
2,400 (crushed from falling debris)
8,840 deaths

NOAA investigators carefully postulated the effects of an 8.3 magnitude earthquake on local medical resources, loss of life, injuries in hospitals, loss of medical and pharmaceutical supplies, as well as damage to hospitals, deaths to health personnel and the capabilities of various bloodbanks and ambulance services. However, no analysis was of greater concern than that dealing with potential deaths and injuries to the student population. In the Bay area, schools of all types are uniformly distributed around the fault zones.

Fortunately, the California public schools have been given special legislative attention because of the disastrous 1933 Long Beach earthquake. Had that temblor occurred during the school day, the potential loss of life would have been appalling. As a result, the California legislature passed the Field Act, making earthquake safety mandatory for all new public school buildings, although it did not prohibit the construction of schools along the active fault zone.

It should be remembered, however, that the newer cities and the suburbs have fewer hazardous structures since they were constructed after 1933.

But as far as schools are concerned, the East Bay presents a special and potentially tragic problem. A total of 31 elementary and secondary schools, including community and state colleges, as well as the University of California at Berkeley are virtually on top of the active Hayward fault. Several of these schools and colleges have their buildings laying across the actual fault trace. During an earthquake, these structures will more than likely be sheared in half. The total population for all 32 schools is 47,752, with nearly 29,000 attending classes within the pre-1933 buildings at the University of California. In sharp contrast, it appears that only one school with a student enrollment of 398 rests on top of the San Andreas fault.

As far as destruction to individual homes is concerned, NOAA estimates that after an 8.3 earthquake hits the Bay area, at least 50 percent of the region will be uninhabitable, since water, gas, and electric utilities will be inoperable, to say nothing of broken windows, doors that won't open and close, etc.

The estimated number of homeless in San Francisco is 19,500 in the event of major fires following the shock. In contrast, 225,000 people were left homeless following the 1906 earthquake and fire. Figures are not available for the number of people who would have to be evacuated below cracked and unsafe dams. The evacuation of these homeless people would pose special problems due to their high concentration in relatively small areas because mass evacuation would be hampered by downed freeways, littered streets and roads, loss of electricity and water, and the lack of nearby accommodations. Obviously, the greatest problems and real hardship cases would occur in the East Bay along the Hayward fault.

The lessons learned from the three days and nights of fire that followed the 1906 shock in San Francisco—which resulted in 80 percent of the property loss—has dominated much of the thinking on the probable effects of the next great San Andreas earthquake. Add to this the 140,000 people killed, injured, and missing in the 1923 Tokyo earthquake and fire and one can sense NOAA's concern for those conflagrations spreading in an uncontrolled manner for a long period of time.

In the event of an 8.3 magnitude shock, no general fire is expected in San Francisco, or in the East Bay, similar to that which occurred in 1906. However, for planning purposes, serious uncontrolled fires are anticipated, although no more than a few city blocks are expected to be lost in these fires. Fires will also probably be restricted to three high-rise buildings.

San Jose and San Mateo, as well as other large cities on the San Francisco Peninsula, will have to anticipate at least one major uncontrolled fire in the industrial areas and one in the residential areas. Except from long distances, mutual aid will not be available. The problems of blocked freeways and broken water lines will create nearly impossible tasks for some fire fighters.

During such uncontrolled conflagrations, the major causes of death will come as fires spread in high-rise buildings. It is reasonable to expect the newest high-rise structures to have more fires due to equipment problems in the middle stories. For example, if a fire should start on the 15th story of a 30-story apartment structure when elevators and stairs are inoperable, deaths in the upper stories could number in the hundreds. Many fire resistive enclosures around elevators and stairs will be shattered and destroyed, allowing fire to climb from story to story where combustible material exists. Obviously, San Francisco would be hardest hit because of the large number of high-rise buildings.

Along the Hayward fault, 15 percent of the water systems will be immediately unavailable, especially for those residents occupying homes in the hills east of the fault. Additionally, no water will flow across the fault due to pipe breakage and over 30 percent of the population will be without water within 12 hours.

Two major uncontrolled fires are expected to occur in the water-short areas: one in Berkeley and the other in Oakland. In addition, it is expected that Berkeley will have many smaller fires, while Oakland will experience huge but controllable fires in the Army and Navy supply areas of the port. The city of Hayward is expected to have several uncontrolled fires for awhile. Life loss in all these fires is not expected to exceed 100 people.

Hardest hit may be the refineries in Richmond and Rodeo. Uncontrolled conflagrations lasting for days and possibly weeks have more than an even chance of occurring.

As far as mass public transportation is concerned, it can be safely assumed that major disruptions will occur along major highway, freeway, railroad, and bridge arteries, as well as at the airport and docking facilities. Extensive damage will come from the collapse of overpasses, partial destruction of bridges crossing the Bay, and slides across roads due to earth failure. Should an 8.3 magnitude earthquake occur during the wet season, landslides will be extensive in the high intensity areas. Marin County is especially vulnerable where the physical volume of the hill areas will prevent quick bulldozer removal or rapid construction of bypasses. Needless to say, major fill areas and embankments will slip or give away.

The bridges which cross the bay pose some very special problems. At the time the Golden Gate and Bay Bridge were designed during the early 1930s, knowledge of earthquake engineering was limited. Even today with new bridges, no high intensity earthquake experience exists to support the theoretical basis for their designs.

Easier to evaluate are the approaches for various bridges. These, of course, turn out to be as critical as those of the bridges during the first few weeks after an earthquake. For example, the land fills in the east approaches of the Bay Bridge appear to be subject to extensive slippage and settlements. The failure of these approach fills would render the bridge inoperable for as long as a week or so. Failure of the elevated interchange structures east of the toll plaza of the Bay Bridge would reduce the bridge's capability. Based on experience in San Fernando's temblor, the elevated approach structures on the west end of the Bay Bridge are also subject to major destruction. But most seismologists agree there is little possibility that either the Bay Bridge or the Golden Gate Bridge will collapse when shaking is at its peak.

Similar problems exist for the San Mateo and Dumbarton Bridges, although much less serious than those for the Bay Bridge. Their miles of trestle allow for quicker temporary repair, although the ship channel areas remain the most vulnerable.

It can be expected that major landslides will block the approaches to the Golden Gate Bridge on the north side, bringing traffic across the span to a halt for days and possibly weeks to come. The actual safety of the great span will always be a controversial question among engineers and seismologists. And, the question of whether or not it will partially or totally collapse in the next great shake will never be fully resolved until the "moment of truth."

Also of controversy among engineers and seismologists is the effect an earthquake of 8.3 magnitude will have on the Bay Area Rapid Transit (BART) tunnel system connecting the East Bay to San Francisco. Seismic hazards to the tube line have been competently analyzed by the best thinking the nation can offer. Special research was conducted on the seismic stability of the underwater muds on the Bay floor. All the records from small earthquakes and their effects on Bay muds were extrapolated ten times over. There is little question that the tube beneath the Bay represents a careful and conservatively designed engineering feat, the best the world has ever known. Yet, no one can reliably quantify all the unpredictable strong motions which Bay muds will experience in a great earthquake of long duration.

Therefore, it must be concluded that the underwater tube is in actuality a carefully conceived experiment. Only time and a major shock will confirm theories of safety. For emergency preparedness planning purposes, the tube under the Bay will be considered out of service for an indefinite period of time.

The BART tunnel through the Berkeley-Oakland hills crossing through the Hayward fault can be expected to cave in along various line points, blocking traffic for months following the shock. Although the system contains special provisions to accommodate fault offset, the tunnel in all likelihood will be shattered, even if the magnitude is as low as 6.0

In summary, then, the two reports provided the Office of Emergency Preparedness and the state of California by the U.S. Department of Commerce's National Oceanic and Atmospheric Administration Environmental Research Laboratories on possible earthquake losses in Los Angeles and San Francisco suggest that planning proceed immediately for relief and recovery from disasters which seismologists say are inevitable.

California's Seismic Seawaves

Californians have some good news in the fact that the coast may be spared the havoc of massive tidal waves because the San Andreas fault slips from side to side instead of up and down. It appears that only certain kinds of earth movements cause significant "tsunamis," seismic sea waves generated by earthquakes, submarine volcanic eruptions or large submarine landslides. The waves are formed in groups and are very long from crest to crest and have a long period. In deep ocean areas, the length of the wave may be a hundred miles or more and wave heights, from crest to trough, may be only a few feet. Tsunamis cannot be felt aboard ships in deep water and normally cannot be seen from the air, but intrinsic wave energies are nonetheless impressive. As a tsunami enters shallower waters along coastlines, wave velocity diminishes and wave height increases. If a trough precedes the initial crest, the arrival of a tsunami is heralded by a gradual recession of coastal water; if a crest precedes, there is a rise in water level. Following this are large waves, some of which can crest at heights of more than 100 feet and strike with devastating force. The worst California can expect from tsunamis was demonstrated by the 1964 tidal wave that hit Crescent City. That wave was set off by the great Alaskan earthquake and caused more than a dozen deaths along the coast. Destroying 200 homes and businesses, it sent cars floating down the streets like battering rams.

Tsunamis, the commonly used Japanese term for seismic or tidal waves, are generally only one or two feet high and 50 miles apart. They travel across the sea at about 400 miles an hour, and their force is felt only when they pile up on a coastline. And, certain harbors "resonate"; that is, they focus the power of the waves to make them stronger and more destructive. Crescent City was a harbor which resonated, while San Francisco Bay is not. Scientists started studying plate tectonics and the ways in which various sections of the earth's crust moved in relation to each other and therefore based tsunami warnings solely on the magnitude of underwater earthquakes. The trouble with the warning system in the past was that scientists had too many warnings for tsunamis that never showed up in significant size. The past systems lost credibility. Today, the basic function of the seismic sea-wave warning system administered by the National Oceanic and Atmospheric Administration is to provide warnings of the approach of potentially damaging tsunamis. The system uses seismographs to detect and locate earthquakes, and tide gauges to detect passing tsunami waves. Automatic alarms are triggered when a tsunami is detected. Methods for determining travel times have been improved so that arrival times now can be predicted to within a minute and a half per elapsed hour. Communication links have been established using the network facilities of the Federal Aviation Agency, Defense Communications Agency, National Aeronautics and Space Administration and the U.S. Weather Bureau. Warning times vary with distances from the source, but periods of several to many hours usually are available to evacuate populations to safe areas.

The earthquake of 1812 was associated with the largest tsunami ever reported in California. The wave may have reached land elevations of 50 feet at Gaviota, California, 30 to 35 feet at Santa Barbara, and 15 or more feet at Ventura.

Most scientists agree that it really is unnecessary for there to be any loss of life due to tsunamis in California. But people can't be foolish. The force of the wave is hard to believe until it hits—and then it's too late. Damage due to tsunamis in California has almost always been greatest at Crescent City in Del Norte County, regardless of points of origin.

The high wave heights at Crescent City perhaps reflect circumstances of exposed coastal location or possibly some unknown peculiarity of bottom topography. The most damaging tsunami of recent years followed the Alaskan earthquake of 1964, and cost the lives of 11 people in Crescent City.

But the ocean waves of death and destruction are not just limited to the Pacific west coast. Every island and coastal settlement in the Pacific Ocean area is vulnerable to the onslaught of seismic sea-waves or the destructive oceanic offspring of underwater earthquakes and volcanic eruption. Mistakenly called "tidal waves" (they are not caused by tides), they have caused tragedy for centuries. In 1868 and 1877, the tsunamis devasted towns in northern Chile and caused death and damage across the Pacific. A series of seismic sea-waves generated by the eruption and collapse of Krakatoa in 1883 killed more than 36,000 in the East Indies. Japan lost 27,000 lives to the wave of 1896, and 1,000 more to that of 1933. There have been hundreds more whose effects were less spectacular but which took many lives and did much damage.

Quake Aftershocks: Unsettled Minds

Psychiatrists have long been interested in the after effects which natural disaster victims develop. Observing that nearly 50 percent of all such victims suffer clearly identifiable forms of neuroses because they lack a sense of purpose or there is no organized assistance to help them after tragedy strikes, psychiatrists have theorized that people can avoid such neurosis if they are made to feel useful immediately after tragedy strikes.

Dr. Alfred Auerback, Professor of Clinical Psychology at the University of California in San Francisco, has been developing a book on the psychic impact of disasters. He writes:

> The trauma of living through an earthquake or flood could affect much of the population, giving them nightmares and feelings of grief, listlessness, guilt, fatigue, depression, and apathy years later. Furthermore, there is absolutely nothing in the entire human experience as frightening as an earthquake. It comes completely without warning. Therefore, there's no way to prepare for it mentally.

According to Auerback and other researchers, earthquakes, like tornadoes, floods, hurricanes and other catastrophic events which affect large numbers of people, leave behind in the unconscious basic physiological "righting reflexes." According to Dr. Merrill Friend, a Sherman Oaks psychiatrist who also teaches for the University of Southern California, "The feeling of having one's feet knocked out from underneath you is very frightening. Many of my patients who survived the San Fernando quakes were immobilized for weeks following the quake whenever an aftershock struck. In a surprising number of cases, marital strain and even divorce began to occur due to feelings of hopelessness about the future or recurring panic."

Psychiatrists have also learned that earthquakes trigger a basic fear of falling. Even among infants, falling seems to be a deep seated aversion which surfaces momentarily in the slightest trembling. Those psychiatric patients who survived the San Fernando earthquake reported months after the event horrible nightmares centering on falling. The mystique that most people carry with them that earthquakes are the deadliest forms to strike civilization add to unconscious anxiety.

Surprisingly, sexual drives are often heightened among earthquake survivors. Also, from a sociological perspective, families tend to draw closer together as social units.

However, the most common behavior noted among two large numbers of San Fernando survivors was "agitative depression," caused after facing the monumental cleanup job which followed. Mothers and children were depressed because of "separation complexes." Youngsters who survived the San Fernando earthquake later drew pictures illustrating their anxieties for parents far from home in great danger. Mothers especially suffered the same separation fears. Researchers also discovered that frequently adults instinctively sought shelter for themselves when the shaking started. Children were ignored during the first few moments. Later, when parents recalled their behavior, they felt immense shame for failing to think of their children first. That deep-rooted guilt has remained with some for years regardless of whether or not their children were hurt.

What can be done to protect people against emotional trauma before and after an earthquake?

Auerback, a member of San Francisco's disaster planning agency, says there is virtually nothing a person can do before a shock. Earthquake rescuers, however, should be conscious that in a major earthquake the need for mental health workers will be almost as great as the need for physicians. According to the psychiatrist, only 25 percent of the survivors will "keep their heads." The rest of the population will need temporary aid. Also, it is important to make sure that people understand why an earthquake has occurred. Then the victims must have something to do in the wake of the disaster, something that will make them feel they are useful.

Auerback feels that the most important thing is the formation of a local group to lend support and help victims deal with government agencies, as well as their own fears. He describes a church organized relief operation in Xenia, Ohio, where a terrifying tornado ripped the town in April of 1974, killing 32 people and causing $100 million dollars in property damage.

Xenia found that people had trouble getting even the bare necessities of life. Those people helped residents get food, blankets, even nails to repair their homes. They served as ombudsmen with government agencies to help iron out red tape and they provided a place where people could talk about their problems. As a result, Xenia is one of the few places to have suffered a recent disaster where the incidence of mental illness had not risen. I predict that San Francisco, sandwiched between the San Andreas and Hayward faults, is certain to suffer another massive earthquake like the one which ruined the city in 1906—a disaster that would leave thousands of people disturbed enough to require prompt attention. But like most Californians, they have learned to live with the threat of quakes by simply ignoring the possibility that they will occur. What real effect such unrealistic thinking has on mental health after a major and devastating earthquake is unknown.

III

Historic Destructions

Throughout the ages, mankind has been terrified and intrigued by earthquake phenomena. Nature's brute strength is never more evident and frightening than when the earth is trembling and shifting. Primitive peoples regarded the sickening sway, the terrible quivering and gaping fissures opening in the ground as acts of a vengeful deity.

Today, earthquakes force us to consider how large and incompletely known our planet is. For example, we inhabit less than one-fourth of its surface and have only explored one-thousandth of its 8,000-mile diameter. Below our shallow grids of cities, roads, tracks, mines and farms lies an unknown, virtually inaccessible, mysterious sphere. Although modern man has visited other planets, he has not penetrated his own. Earthquakes never let us forget this fact. Since long before man existed, probably for more than 4½ billion years, the forces within the earth which have caused these earthquakes have played an active role in shaping the earth's surface. These unpredictable catastrophic movements of the earth have caused great human casualties, suffering, and property damage.

Most natural hazards can be detected before their threat kills. But *seisms* (from the Greek word for "trembling earth," *seismos*) have no known precursors. Indeed, they arrive suddenly without warning, like the vengeance of an ancient, depraved god. For this reason, they continue to devastate—over 650,000 people killed in China alone in 1976. These deaths did not occur in antiquity. Furthermore, those who survive the horror of a lethal quake must somehow survive fire, pestilence, looting, fear, homelessness, and the economic burden of rebuilding while an indifferent planet continues its spinning.

Today, man is challenging the assumption that these earthquakes must present an uncontrollable and unpredictable hazard to life and property.* Scientists have begun to explore the means of predicting earthquakes, sites of greatest hazard are being identified, and history being analyzed to uncover mistakes which might aid architects in designing structures which will withstand the effects of earthquakes.

As we now know, earthquakes are the result of very slow geological processes and we need a very long period of observation before we can deduce the laws that govern them.

In spite of the large amount of data on earthquakes in this century, the period of observation is too short. After all, the scientific study of earthquakes is comparatively new. To increase this period one has to resort to the study of earthquakes that took place before this century and to choose regions which have a long and well-recorded history.

World Seismic History

Until the 18th century, few factual descriptions of earthquakes were recorded and their natural cause was little un-

---

*In 1906, the San Francisco earthquake did an estimated $24 million property damage, and the ensuing fire $500 million more. Since that time, Americans have paid another $600 million for earthquake damage, approximately $375 million to the 1964 Alaskan earthquake. In the past 77 years, the average annual toll has run $20 million. Needless to say, a major earthquake in a large metropolitan center would change these figures drastically and there is every reason to believe other seismic disasters lie ahead of us.

derstood. Most believed that a trembling earth was massive punishment and a warning to the unrepentant. For example, a 15th century scholar suggested that statues of Mercury and Saturn be placed on each wall of buildings to protect against earthquakes. Those who did look for natural causes often reached fanciful conclusions; one popular theory was that earthquakes were caused by air rushing out of caverns deep in the earth's interior.

One area of the globe which has a very long and well-documented history is China. Scientists in that country, studying reliable historical records over the past three millennia, have recently made significant progress in predicting regions in China where earthquakes are likely to be destructive.

The long Chinese records show significant and surprising temporal variations which are barely hinted at in the much shorter seismic histories that characterize most other parts of the world. For example, two of the Chinese historic events (1556 Shensi and 1920 Kansu) are among the most gigantic natural disasters of world history. It is little wonder that the historic records of early seismic events in China have come under close scrutiny in the effort to plan intelligently for the future.

The first comprehensive modern catalog of Chinese earthquakes seems to have been prepared in the mid-1950s in response to the need for earthquake information on economic developments such as new mining districts. A new edition of the catalog was published in 1971, and even further additions and corrections have been made since that time. The principal effort for collecting and cataloging the information has been by the Academia Sinica, the Institute of Geophysics, and the Institute of History. Their principal source for information has been the local gazetters and records of local historians. Ever since the time of the Yin Dynasty (1532–1028 B.C.), official historians wrote not only of political affairs, but also of natural phenomena which could be regarded as portents. The first earthquake on record is that of 1831 B.C., although regular listings in the

1971 catalog begin with the event of 1177 B.C. Chinese seismologists have assigned epicentral coordinates and magnitudes to some 1,323 individual earthquakes from that time to the present, apparently selected from more than 9,000 documented shocks. The impressive wealth of data available on distribution of damage is indicated by the fact that 146 isoseismal maps* are illustrated in the catalog, including events as early as the damaging earthquake in A.D. 138 near Lanchow, Kansu. Some 629 earthquakes are said to have had a magnitude of 6.0 or greater, 95 events between 7.0 and 7.9, and 18 of magnitude 8.0 and more.

The Chinese historical data before 1900 show almost no epicenters of large earthquakes in the Tibet and Sinkiang regions. Yet, the post-1900 instrumental record shows a great quantity of current seismic activity occurring in this region, with almost none in the area of eastern China, the primary focus of much of the earlier historic records. Although it is possible that the locus of seismic activity changed with time, a far more logical conclusion is simply that the extremely low population density in western China resulted in much earth movement going unnoticed or unrecorded.

On the other hand, northern China, the cradle of Chinese civilization, has a remarkably complete record of large earthquakes dating back to about 466 B.C., particularly in the Fen and Wei River valleys. Records illustrate that the region is homogeneous, with magnitudes of about 5 for all the earthquakes since 1484.

The truly remarkable catalog of Chinese earthquakes was partially aided by 5,600 individual local gazetteers. And, at that, four major difficulties were encountered by the Chinese researchers: (1) problems due to changes in calendar systems in the various dynasties, accurate dates being hard to establish, and duplications difficult to avoid; (2) locations often hard to pin down because of obscure or changed area

---

*Maps that relate to earthquake shocks of equal intensity.

names, because of this there has been an unfortunate tendency to place earthquakes at capitals or other major cities; (3) some records have obviously gross exaggerations; and (4) many earthquakes have inadequate descriptions. The five most important earthquakes in Chinese history, according to the Chinese catalog are listed as follows:

1. The great 1303 Hung-tsao (Shansi) earthquake occurred in the Fen River valley between Sian and Taiyuan, an area that has had much recurring seismicity throughout the historic record. Forty-seven counties recorded the 1303 event, 34 with destruction. . . . The magnitude is given as 8 on the basis of Chinese formulas (which vary from region to region) relating intensity to magnitude.

2. The 1556 Huahsien (Shensi) earthquake may qualify as the greatest natural disaster in history. Well-documented deaths reportedly exceeded 820,000, and the destructive area was some 870 km long. It was reported in 212 counties (98 with destruction) in 8 provinces. In the 6 counties within the most heavily shaken area, the average death rate in villages was 60 percent almost all due to colapsing houses at night. . . . The magnitude is thought to be between 8.0 and 8.3, and the depth of focus is calculated as 24 km. The hundred years prior to the event was generally marked by high to moderate seismic activity in the epicentral region, except that a quiet period immediately preceded the earthquake for about 13 years. There was only one damaging aftershock, in 1558.

3. The great Tanch'eng or Lienshui (Shantung) earthquake of 1668 was unusual and disconcerting in that it occurred in a part of eastern China, about halfway between Shanghai and Peking, that has neither before nor since been one of continuing high activity. And it was preceded by a period of more than 150 years of almost total quiescence in the epicentral region. The earthquake was recorded in 379 counties, 29 of which had 'heavy destruction'; three county seats were completely destroyed. Following the earthquake until 1900, the epicentral region

was the locus of a modest number of small earthquakes, but there is now some concern that since 1900 the area has again become one of almost total seismic quiescence. . . [It is perhaps significant that the epicenter of the very recent destructive earthquake of February 1975, which occurred subsequent to the visit of the American delegation, was located in Liaoning Province some 700 km farther north and apparently along the same Quaternary fault system as that of the 1668 event. Similarly, the area of the 1975 earthquake does not appear to have been characterized by major preceding historic seismic activity.]

4. In 1679, Peking was severely shaken by a great earthquake centered some 50–60 km from the city. Contemporary poems hint at numerous fissures within the city. Peking was also damaged by smaller but destructive shocks in 1057, 1337, 1484, 1536, 1658, 1665, and 1730, but none since. A dense telemetered seismic network in operation since 1966 shows that numerous small earthquakes ($M = 1.8–3.5$) tend to occur in roughly the same places as the earlier larger shocks. . .

5. The 1920 Haiyuan (Kansu) earthquake of magnitude 8.5 is the largest earthquake in contemporary China and has been the subject of several articles in the modern literature. The great loss of life was in part associated with massive soil failures in the thick loess that blankets the Kansu region. A 200-km-long left lateral fault associated with the earthquake has recently been reported. Perhaps the most significant aspect of the earthquake is that the region outlined by aftershocks has been almost totally quiescent for 280 years prior to 1920, although it clearly lies within a broad zone of longer historic activity.

To seismologists all over the world, the great significance of the historic record of Chinese earthquakes lies in its implications for the use of these records in seismic zoning and for statistical extrapolations of expected future activity. The principal lesson to be learned is that even a 3,000-year-old record must be used with extreme caution in extropolating into the future, since it is clearly statistically inadequate in many ways. For other parts of the world where historical records of seismic activity are less than a tenth as long as that of China, the lesson is even more dramatic. The basic problem is simply that seismicity is not uniform in time and space even during periods as long as 3,000 years and in regions as large as China itself.

* * *

In the eastern hemisphere, another region which has a long and well-documented history is the area between Italy and Afghanistan. This area is currently under study by Imperial College in London, the object being to extract from old documents information about early events that could throw some light on the mechanisms that produce earthquakes, on the manner in which such events migrate and, in general, on the evaluation of the earthquake risk in this part of the world.

The basic data for this study is being retrieved from published and unpublished documents, local histories and inscriptions written in Greek, Latin, Syriac, Persian, Arabic, Slavonic, Georgian and Turkish, as well as from the field study of early earthquake sites. This is a long-term interdisciplinary project originally supported by the United Nations.

In these studies, archaeological evidence is very important, particularly in regions for which written evidence is either inconclusive or scarce. Surprisingly, such subjects as numismatics play a significant role in assessing the destructiveness of early earthquakes, as the issue of new coinage and the establishment of new mints were often measures taken by the authorities to relieve regions after disastrous earthquakes.

Inscriptions recording public assistance and private generosity for the reconstruction of destroyed towns are equally valuable. Abrupt changes in building materials and methods of construction as well as the location of settlements are all useful in assessing the relative importance of early earthquakes.

When evaluating historic seismic activity, other factors have also to be taken into consideration. Among these are population density; uniformity and concordance of source material; natural exaggeration in the description of early earthquakes; and the varying attitudes of historians and poets throughout the ages to phenomena such as earthquakes, which reflect the importance they attach to the events they are recording.

One of the major aspects of the research is the identification of large earthquakes and the rate at which they have been occurring during the last 2,000 years. Another is the assessment of their economic and social impact on the people in the region and their effect on the environment.

The search for large earthquakes is not limited to the most populous centers. It is usually possible to determine that an earthquake felt in large towns, where it may be well-documented, was felt even more severely and destructively in outlying, less cultivated areas nearer to the true epicenter, where some cloistered sage may have referred to it in the course of a voluminous history of his sect of township, or in a panegyric on his local ruler.

Large earthquakes can be identified from the size of the area over which they were felt, the duration of their after-shocks, the degree of damage wrought in the center of the earthquake area and from the economic and social impact they have on those involved.

There is little doubt about the size of the earthquake of July 21, A.D. 365, which affected an area of about two million square kilometers in the eastern Mediterranean, between Italy and Palestine, and Greece and North Africa. This earthquake, one of the dozen that have shaken the eastern Mediterranean during the last two and a half milennia, was associated with a catastrophic sea-wave which in Alexandria alone drowned 5,000 people. Evidence of the social impact this earthquake had is found in the church calendar. For two centuries the event was commemorated in Egypt and Greece by a yearly festival meant to appease the sea and arrest the waves, which in A.D. 365 carried boats over the walls of towns and deposited them on roof tops, drowning thousands of people.

Recent archaeological evidence has shown the effects of the A.D. 365 disaster which marked the end of a number of declining towns in Libya and Sicily. Hoards of coins found on the floor of public buildings trapped by the tumbled down masses of masonry pre-date the disaster and testify to the abandonment of these sites.

Evidence of catastrophic earthquakes abound in areas which today appear to be free from earthquakes. North-central Iran is a typical example. During the last two millennia, sites such as Shahr-Reyy, today a suburb of Tehran, Qumis near modern Semnan, Nishapur and Juvain not far from Mashhad, and other places in Khorassan, were totally destroyed and abandoned.

Indeed, Shahr-Reyy was well-known for its earthquakes even during the time of Alexander the Great; the Greek name of the locality *Rhagae* meant a place "rent in an earthquake." Elsewhere, destructive earthquakes in Baluchistan and Oman, in Lebanon and western Syria, as well as near Kabul and Rawalpindi are known to have caused widespread damage.

In many instances, particularly in the western part of the area being studied, official documents of the late Roman and Byzantine periods give lists of towns that after destructive earthquakes received financial assistance from the government, as well as remission of all contributions to the exchequer for a number of years to help their reconstruction. These lists make it possible today to assess the extent of the area affected by early earthquakes.

The earliest written evidence requesting such action was actually found in tablets from northern Iraq, dating back to the later part of the second millenium B.C. This particular request came from an ill-defined region north of Mosul, which today is considered to be almost free from large earthquakes. Similar second millenium B.C. notices have been found referring to the inability of the local rulers to pay taxes after destructive earthquakes on the Mediterranean coasts and in Syria.

To earthquake researchers, a fascinating question has now come up. Could legendary Atlantis have been an island in the Mediterranean which sunk during a major earthquake? That is, can the disappearance of the famed continent of Atlantis, described by Plato in his *Dialogues* and the subject of so much controversy and theorizing, be explained in terms of an ancient seismic catastrophe in the Aegean Sea? Some archaeologists believe so, or at least believe that the seismic history of the eastern Mediterranean can throw light on the sudden collapse, around 1500 B.C. of the Minoan empire and the Cretan civilization, one of the greatest of antiquity.

Scientists now know that 3,500 years ago the eastern Mediterranean was the scene of one of history's most gigantic natural disasters: the explosion (around 1480 B.C.) of the volcanic island of Santorin, 100 km north of Crete. The explosion sent millions of tons of volcanic ash hurtling into the atmosphere, giving rise to intense atmospheric shocks and generating devastating tidal waves that destroyed many ports and towns of the Minoan empire.

Examining this cataclysm and the theories that have been put forward about it, notably by Professor Spyridon Marinatos, director of the Greek Department of Antiquities, George Pararas-Carayannis, Director of the International Tidal Wave Information Center in Honolulu, says: "Recent archaeological work on the island of Santorin unearthed, partly submerged below the sea, a completely intact 3,500-year-old Minoan city. Excavations by the University of Athens uncovered one, two, and three-story houses and numerous Minoan artifacts and utensils. The absence of human skeletons from the city indicates that the inhabitants had advance warning of the oncoming eruption of the volcano and had time to evacuate the island.'' The volcanic eruption and the tidal wave alone did not entirely destroy the Minoan civilization, but for two centuries the Minoan civilization on Crete was weakened by numerous earthquakes that destroyed its cities and caused it to decline rapidly. As for the legend of Atlantis, he concluded, ''Whether Santorin and the other Minoan colonies on the Aegean islands actually constituted the lost continent of Atlantis may never be known with absolute certainty.''

But the key evidence in determining the damaging effects of ancient earthquakes remains the deterioration of the local coinage taken together with other evidence. This was the case, for instance, in the A.D. 25 earthquake which destroyed Taxila, in northern Pakistan, very near modern Islamabad. The earthquake destroyed the mint and apparently killed its engravers. Similar cases have been found for Rhodes, Cyprus, and western Anatolia.

After the Taxila earthquake, houses were rebuilt stronger, with special precautions to make their foundations secure. In some cases these were carried down as much as five meters, a drastic change in building techniques also noticed elsewhere, notably in western and southern Anatolia and Syria, where after destructive earthquakes, builders reduced the height of new houses from three to one or two stories and the lower story was left half buried beneath the fallen debris, and thus constituted a sort of basement.

After destructive earthquakes, towns were often rebuilt on an extensive plan with marked changes in building techniques such as unusual types of foundations, consisting of a grid of wooden beams on which the structures were built, the introduction of timber-bracing of houses and the abandonment of ordinary unreinforced brickwork. It is often assumed that these changes are due to techniques brought into the region by new settlers, or by invaders. However, this is not always the case.

The acknowledged advantages of timber-braced construction in regions subject to earthquakes have conditioned building methods (for instance in Anatolia, Crete, northern Pakistan and elsewhere), up to quite recent times. Historical as well as archaeological evidence shows that even in antiquity such a device was intended to give to a building resilience that would increase its resistance to earthquakes, although it would decrease its fire resistance. What puzzles archaeologists is the use of timber-bracing as a building technique in areas situated outside the regions where earthquakes are most prevalent today.

Studies of areas that have been damaged or devastated repeatedly by earthquakes follow not only a well-defined pattern, but also indicate that this pattern, in places, fits surprisingly well that of earthquakes that occurred during this century.

However, studies also show that quakes occurred in regions which today are thought to be free from large earthquakes, such as the Dead Sea, southeast Turkey, northern Syria and Iraq, and the central Balkans and eastern Iran. Study shows that zones which were notorious for their destructive earthquakes, such as those in northern Syria and Iraq or east-central Iran, are quiescent today, while zones which are active today, such as Anatolia and the Zagros, were free from large earthquakes two generations ago.

Individual zones may undergo long periods of activity followed by equally long periods of inactivity, lasting many generations, during which precautionary measures against earthquakes in building houses are gradually abandoned only to be taken up again a few hundred years later. As was said earlier, the human time-scale is minutely short when compared with the time-scale involved in the geological processes leading to the quakes.

In contrast with wars, epidemics, and other long-lasting calamities, earthquakes, no matter how large, seem to have had little long-term impact on man. Personal, religious and in particular economic interests seem to overshadow the lessons to be learned from earthquakes.

Antiochia, the modern Antakya in Turkey, is a good example. Since it was founded, the city, built partly on very soft ground, had suffered from earthquakes. In A.D. 115, the city was almost totally destroyed, but because of its strategic position it was rebuilt on the same site. In A.D. 458, Antiochia was almost totally destroyed by another earthquake and rebuilt on the same spot although it was pointed out to those concerned that reconstruction on the same site was likely to be unwise.

The part of the city on the worst ground, on the river, being settled by merchants, was of course rebuilt, only to be totally destroyed a generation later with the loss of 200,000 lives. Antiochia was again rebuilt on the same site, this time becoming an important religious center, and was finally destroyed in A.D. 540 by the Persians.

The economic effects that an earthquake may have on a developing country or on a poor community are more important and they can lead to serious and often uncontrollable disasters, far more important than the immediate destructive effects of an earthquake. The damage and sudden crippling of an unstable economy may lead to population movements, to a latent emigration of skilled people, increase in taxation and to undesirable, though unavoidable, loans from foreign countries which may lead to economic and social consequences. For instance, as early as the 5th century B.C. an earthquake in Sparta gave the opportunity to the subject Helots to shake off the yoke of their Spartan masters. In A.D. 978 an earthquake marked the end of Siraf, a declining port on the Persian Gulf. In A.D. 1139, Gandja, the former Elizavetpol, now Kirovabad, was destroyed by an earthquake in which more than 100,000 people perished; this gave the Georgians an opportunity to sack the ruined city.

The earthquakes of 1157 in Syria caused great damage, killing thousands of people. They brought about a temporary peace between Moslems and Crusaders who were too busy repairing shattered forts to think of serious aggressive expeditions for some time to come; these earthquakes, however, caused little change in the final outcome of the Crusades.

An earthquake in 1320 completely destroyed Ani the capital of the Armenian province of Ararat, causing its inhabitants to disperse into various parts of the world, as far as Poland and Iran. The real cause for the desertion of the ruined city, however, was the decadence of the Mongol dynasty in Armenia.

In 1755, the Lisbon earthquake, on the other hand, provided an opportunity for the rebuilding of the city on a grand scale and also for reducing the trading privileges of foreigners, thus stimulating an already active economy. Occurring on November 1, shocks from this massive earthquake were felt in many parts of the world. Even in some areas of the United States, chandeliers rattled. In every corner of Europe, buildings trembled. An eyewitness wrote:

> The sea rose boiling in the harbour and broke up all the craft harboured there. The city burst into flames, and ashes covered the streets and squares, the houses came crushing down, roofs piling up on foundations, and even the foundations were smashed to pieces. Thirty thousand inhabitants were crushed to death under the ruins.

After this devastating quake, Portugese priests were asked to document their observations. Their records are still preserved and represent the first systematic attempt to investigate an earthquake and its effects. Since then, detailed records have been kept of almost every major earthquake.

What did early man believe caused the devastating earthquakes?

The ancient Japanese believed that the hundreds of quakes that shook (and still shake) their islands every year were caused by the casual movements of a giant spider who carried the earth on his back. Later, the Japanese felt it was not so much a giant spider as a dragon with a lion's head, eagle's talons, and serpent's tail which made the earth "quake" when it bestirred itself. The serpent hid in the caverns of inaccessible mountains or lay coiled as a giant catfish in the ocean depths waiting for the moment to unite earth and water in a huge explosion. Symbolized in it were nature's energies and the beginning of new life. Unlike the malevolent dragon of the West, the dragon in the East was the genius of goodness and strength. It was the spirit of change, therefore of life itself. And nothing demonstrated its power better than an earthquake when it ascended from the skies and mountains and buried itself in the watery depths of Japan's coasts.

Natives of Siberia's quake-prone Kamchatka Peninsula blamed the tremors on a giant dog named Kosei tossing snow off his fur. Pythogoras, the Greek philosopher and mathematician, believed that earthquakes were caused by the dead fighting among themselves. Another ancient Greek, Aristotle, had a more scientific explanation. He insisted that the earth's rumblings were the result of hot air masses trying to escape from the earth's interior. Plato had an equally mistaken notion. He contended that earthquakes were caused by powerful subterranean winds.

On the American continent, the Algonquin Indians believed that when the earth shook it meant the Great Tortoise, who supported the world, was shifting his weight.

As late as 1750, Thomas Sherlock, the Bishop of London, preached to his flocks that two recent earthquakes were warnings that Londoners should atone for their sins. John Wesley agreed. In a 1777 letter to a friend, he wrote: "There is no divine visitation which is likely to have so general an influence upon sinners as an earthquake . . .".

There is little question that along with war and pestilence earthquakes rank as one of the world's most feared killers. Striking without warning and opening great fissures in mankind's ultimate sanctuary of terra firma, quakes have inspired terror and awe since man first walked the earth. During recorded history, earthquakes, along with the floods, fires, and landslides they have triggered, are estimated to have taken as many as 75 million lives.

Global Distribution of Earthquake Belts

It has long been recognized that earthquakes tend to be confined almost exclusively within certain well-defined zones of mountain-building, active volcanoes, island arcs with adjacent deep-ocean trenches, and oceanic ridges. Epicenters occur chiefly in these few narrow belts or zones. Seismologically speaking, the most important subdivisions of the earth's surface are:

1) The circum-Pacific belt, with many branches.
2) The Alpide belt of Europe and Asia, considered an extension of one of the main branches of the circum-Pacific belt.
3) The Pamir-Baikal zone of central Asia.
4) The Atlantic-Arctic belt.
5) The belt of the central Indian ocean, with several branches.
6) Rift zones, notably those of East Africa.
7) A wide triangular active area in eastern Asia, between the Alpide belt and the Pamir-Baikal zone.
8) Minor seismic areas, usually in regions of older mountain-building.
9) The central basin of the northern Pacific Ocean, almost non-seismic except for the Hawaiian Island.
10) The stable central shields of the continents, also nearly non-seismic.

A globe with such seismic belts or zones resembles a jigsaw puzzle. Each conforms to a general pattern. The Australian piece, for example, centers naturally about the old land of west Australia. The edges of the piece to the north

HISTORY'S MOST AWESOME EARTHQUAKES

YEAR	AREA	DEATH TOLL
373	Helice, Greece	Unknown
856	Corinth, Greece	45,000
1556	Shensi, China	830,000
1707	Tokyo, Japan	Unknown
1737	Calcutta, India	300,000
1755	Lisbon, Portugal	60,000
1783	Italy	Unknown
1883	Dutch Indies	36,000
1902	Martinique	40,000
1906	San Francisco	700
1908	Italy	73,000
1915	Italy	29,000
1920	Kansu, China	180,000
1923	Tokyo	143,000
1927	China	200,000
1932	China	70,000
1935	Pakistan	40,000
1939	Turkey	23,000
1953	Greece	3,000
1960	Agadir, Morocco	12,000
1960	Chile	5,700
1962	Iran	12,200
1963	Yugoslavia	1,200
1964	Alaska	114
1966	Turkey	2,500
1968	Iran	12,000
1970	Peru	67,000
1972	Iran	5,400
1972	Managua, Nicaragua	10,000
1975	Mudken, China	*
1976	Guatemala	22,000
1976	China	650,000
1977	Bucharest, Roumania	4,000

*Unreported, but believed to be high.

and east follow the circum-Pacific belt through the East Indies and down to New Zealand; the other edges are the active zones of the Indian Ocean which separate this piece from those of India, Africa, and Antarctica.

In many parts of the circum-Pacific belt and some segments of the Alpine—Himalayan belt, the earthquakes are contained within narrow Benioff zones (named in honor of the late Hugo Benioff at the California Institute of Technology). These zones dip downward along inclined planes beneath the continental margins to depths as great as 700 km. In other sections of these belts, such as along the San Andreas fault, the earthquakes occur along nearly vertical planes which extend downward into the earth's crust for only a few tens of kilometers. The earthquakes in the mid-oceanic ridge belt are shallow and occur near the ridge crests.

IV

Why Earthquakes Happen

What really happens when the earth trembles violently and the ground opens? Scientists are still not sure, although they have theories rooted to powerful prehistoric forces in both the universe and our own restless, hot-hearted planet.

For the pyrotechnics of continents being pushed around, with the building of mountain ranges and the opening and closing of oceans, seismologists must first gaze across the vast vault of the sky for answers. In the array of billions upon billions of stars, they have discovered many fantastic properties: stars that gleam ten trillion times more brightly than the sun, objects so dense a teaspoonful would weigh as much as 600 million automobiles, mysterious black holes whose incredible gravitational pull sucks in the dust and stuff of space never to be seen again. Scientists have cataloged that jumbled throng of stars into an orderly sequence by variety and age, as if they had looked at a crowd of people and sorted them into infants, children, young adults, the middle-aged, and the elderly.

Astronomers calculate that the oldest stars formed with the universe itself about 13 billion years ago when a primordial mass exploded with a titanic bang, sending particles flying in every direction. These clouds of gas and matter have been condensing ever since to form galaxies of stars and planets. Some 4.6 billion years ago, scientists believe, our own planet coalesced from such a swirling nebula of gas and dust. As gravity pulled the mass together, collisions, compression, and radioactivity heated it until temperatures at the center reached millions of degrees. Hydrogen atoms fused to form helium, kindling a source of energy—nuclear fusion—that has kept the sun ablaze ever since. It has fuel enough to continue for billions of years more.

The condensing solar cloud spawned orbiting bodies of various sizes. These collided and accumulated until there grew the planets and satellites known today. Meteorites strike the earth as that collection progress still goes on. From analysis and dating of these extraterrestrial rocks, along with other clues read in the heavens, scientists conclude that the composition of the solar system is remarkably uniform— persuasive arguments for a common origin 4.6 million years ago.

The oldest known earth-rocks, discovered in Greenland, dated back 3.8 million years. Rocks nearly as old have been found in Minnesota, Labrador, and South Africa. All resemble the youngest of rocks, suggesting that the earth was not very different in composition then from now. Older ones may turn up, but one explanation for the age difference between meteorites and the oldest rock may be that the earth took a long time to form. Evidently it passed through a molten stage, as it cooled, heavier matter rich in iron settled to the center, lighter rocks like basalt and granite rose to the surface, eventually forming a crust. Volcanoes brought gases and water vapor from deep within to create an atmosphere and the seas and continents developed. The earth took shape.

So far this is a familiar description; but a new view of the world and its workings suggests that our seemingly fixed earth is always changing. Continents drift about—bumping into each other to thrust up mountains, breaking apart to shape new lands. As the earth retches and steam and exploding lava streak the skies, ocean basins appear and disappear. These awesome events take eons, but the earth in its own slow way is a very dynamic body.

This concept—that oceans and continents are not fixed and permanent but that lands are mobile and seas ephemeral—constitutes one of history's great leaps in scientific understanding. Because of it, old ideas have been overturned, old textbooks have had to be rewritten. It has done for earthquake thinking what Copernicus's realization of a sun-centered solar system did for astronomy, what Darwin's theory of evolution did for biology, what Einstein's theory of relativity did for physics. It is a true scientific revolution. And, it only occurred in the 1960s.

Therefore, today's most widely accepted theory holds that earthquakes are caused by the titanic shifts in the crust along crack or fracture lines called faults. Portions of the crust are under constant stress, like a bent bow. At frequent intervals, when the strain becomes intolerable, the rock gives way at some weak point, often far beneath the surface. Because of this, our layered planet's brittle rind becomes awesomely scarred.

A simplified cross section of the earth would show four regions: inner and outer cores totaling some 4,000 miles in radius and believed to be largely iron and nickel. The inner core has a diameter of 1,600 miles with temperatures up to 10,800° F while the outer core's molten metal thickness is estimated to be 1,800 miles, reaching temperatures of 7,300° F. These are followed by a mantle of rock, about 1,400 miles thick, which is neither liquid nor solid. The mantle is probably composed of a plastic-like igneous rock which yields or flows with infinite slowness under pressure. Temperatures range from 1,300° to 5,000° F. Finally, a solid, generally brittle, outer crust composed largely of basalt overlaid with granite and sediments touches the surface. Like the shell of an egg, the crust's thickness under the oceans is from 3 to 7 miles; under the continents, it's thickness is 15 to 35 miles.

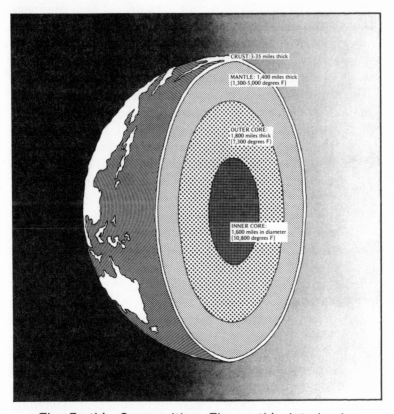

The Earth's Composition. The earth's interior is comprised of a solid inner core and a liquid outer core, encased in a mantle, covered by a crust which varies in thickness from five to forty miles.

As the thickness of this crust makes sudden shifts, it releases pent-up energy in enormously powerful waves which cause the whole world to vibrate like a giant bell. Most of these waves circle the globe while others pass completely through the earth at speeds of 3 to 8 miles per second. All these waves record their passing in the jiggling of pens on sensitive measuring instruments called seismographs.

Thus, we see that our vibrant planet has a layered structure. Seismic waves from explosive charges or from the tens of thousands of quakes that shake the earth every year help tell us so. Some of these waves pass through liquids, others cannot. Boundaries between layers bend certain kinds of waves, reflect others. Speeds vary as the waves travel through different types of material. From this and other evidence, we conclude that our planet somewhat resembles a soft-boiled egg—it has a thin, brittle, shell-like crust and a thick, solid section called the mantle, representing the white, and a partly liquid core equivalent to the yolk.

Earth's original heat and the energy from decay of radioactive elements are thought to keep the interior at temperatures of perhaps 8,000° F. The core, like the charge of a blast furnace, is largely liquid iron, but great pressure at the very center compresses a dense inner core to solid iron. The mantle is rigid and consists of iron-rich silicate rocks. Like the lining of a blast furnace, these silicates do not melt as easily as iron. Pressure keeps the lower part of the mantle hard; higher up, the hot rock becomes slightly plastic. This layer is called the asthenosphere (from the Greek *asthenes* for "weak"). Nearer the surface the earth is cooler and becomes more rigid again, forming the layer called the lithosphere, from *lithos* for "stone." This includes the top of the mantle and the entire crust—the latter averaging some 21 miles thick under continents and about 3 miles under ocean basins.

Realization that the lithosphere and asthenosphere differ in their resistance to deformation provided an understanding of how continents drift. The asthenosphere behaves like a pliable, red-hot poker—or, like ice, which in a cube from one's refrigerator is crystalline and brittle, but in a mass as large as a glacier can shift and flow. This was first appreciated when it was observed that the asthenosphere can yield under loads. Glacial sheets of the ice age weighted down the land; measurements show that much of North America has risen since they melted. Continents, formed of relatively light rocks, can float high on the asthenosphere, but the heavier basalt of ocean floors cannot. The continents can wander about, for the new view of an ever-changing earth holds that the lithosphere is cracked into huge plates which move over the layer below.

Where plates separate, molten rock wells up, cooking and solidifying to form new crust. Elsewhere, plates are pushed together and one may be forced beneath another to soften and merge in the hot depths. This theory can explain how mountains are formed, what causes earthquakes and volcanic eruptions, why Antarctica once had fern forests—questions inadequately explained by old ideas. Piecing the theory together has been one of the best detective stories in the history of science.

Almost as soon as outlines of the new world began to appear on maps, imaginations were provoked by the jigsaw-puzzle fit of opposite coasts of the Atlantic. In 1782, Benjamin Franklin wondered if "the surface of the globe would be a shell" capable of swimming on an internal fluid. Other scientists held that the old and new worlds had been rent asunder by a cataclysmic event, probably involving the flood described in the Bible. Then in 1908 an American geologist, Frank B. Taylor, proposed that the continents were moving about slowly, propelled by tidal action. And by 1912, the German meteorologist, Alfred Wegener, had marshalled arguments to support the first comprehensive view of continents in motion.

Wegener not only showed that the edges of the continental shelves moved but he also demonstrated that rocks and fossils on opposite shores of the Atlantic dovetail remarkably. "It is just as if we were to refit the torn pieces of a newspaper . . . and then check whether the lines of print run smoothly across it. If they do, there is nothing left but to conclude that the pieces were in fact joined in this way," he wrote. He argued that if continents can move vertically, it is logical to suppose that they can also move laterally. He cited evidence of great climactic changes: fossils of subtropical forests in now-Arctic Spitzbergen, salt beds from seas that dried when North America must have lain in the torrid zone, debris left by glaciers in lands now near the equator.

But Wegener's suggestion that stone continents plow through stone floors of the oceans like stately ships seemed too preposterous to accept. Sir Harold Jeffreys, then the world's most influential geophysicist, spurned the drift theory as "quantitatively insufficient and qualitatively inapplicable." Other scientists used minor flaws in the argument to deride the concept. When Wegener died in 1930 of a casualty on a hazardous meteorological expedition into the middle of the Greenland ice cap, few persons had accepted his unorthodox views.

For a quarter of a century, Wegener's theory has been largely ignored. The discoveries made after World War II by the application of new scientific devices forced a renewed interest. Echo sounders using principles designed to detect submarines gave exact charts of ocean floors. Magnometers were devised that could be towed on the ocean surface to record weak magnetism in rock beneath the ooze miles below. Instruments were designed to pinpoint the source of earthquakes, to make delicate readings of gravity, to measure heat flow from the earth's interior—it was as if earth's skin at last could be peeled back for a look at what lay beneath. Until then, earth scientists had been like doctors of old who, lacking stethoscope or x-ray, could examine only the outsides of their patients.

But proof that continents are in motion did not come immediately, as an inspriation in the mind of one genius. Evidence built up piece by piece. Each advance had to struggle against entrenched ideas; each scientist had to abandon cherished views.

As late as 1960, geologists and members of the American Geophysical Union were still skeptical. Not until after 1965 was evidence clear enough to win over most doubters in the scientific community. Two broad areas of investigation provided the strongest support. One involved study of magnetic records frozen in ancient rocks—paleomagnetism. The other was tracing an underwater mountain system that winds about the globe.

Until a century ago, scientists knew virtually nothing about the floors of the oceans except that they were very deep. Then soundings compiled by Matthew Fontaine Maury, a U.S. Naval officer, and by the British exploration ship *Challenger* revealed the presence of an underwater ridge bisecting the Atlantic. In time, other expeditions found other ridges in other seas. By 1956, Maurice Ewing and Bruce C. Heezen, professors at Columbia University, could show that all the ridges are connected into a single mighty mountain range, sprawling as much as 3,000 miles wide.

Thus, cracked into a score of pieces, the earth's lithosphere includes our familiar crust of continents and ocean basins. Literally, stone ships sail over the seas of time at rates of up to a few inches per year. Ponderously slow churnings in the semi-plastic interior are thought to drive the plates in endless driftings. These plates are known as the Eurasian, Philippine, Pacific, Indo-Australian, American, Caribbean, Cocos, Nazca, Antarctic, African, Arabian, and Somali Plates. Where plate edges grind together, earthquakes most frequently occur. Where plates split apart, molten rock may surge to the surface and solidify; one great rift along which this happens meanders about the globe for 40,000 miles. In certain "subduction" zones, the edge of one plate dips below another—to melt in the depths and breed volcanoes. In other "transform faults," regions of plates slip sideways past each other.

Scientists believe plate movements have carried the continents across the face of the earth since early in history. Two hundred million years ago all were joined in one huge mass which got the name *Pangaea,* meaning "all lands," from the writings of Alfred Wegener, the father of the continental drift theory. Pangaea was washed by a universal ocean—*Panthalassa,* "all seas." But 135 million years ago, Pangaea divided into northern Laurasia and southern Gondwana, with an embryo Mediterranean between them, and India and an Australia-Antarctica split off. About 65 million years ago the Atlantic had developed and India drove toward Asia, eventually to bump up the Himalayas.

Today, ocean-floor spreading shoves North America farther from Europe by an inch a year; parts of the Pacific creep* four times as fast. In 50 million years, if movements continue unchanged, Africa will have begun to break apart, the Mediterranean will be squeezed into a large lake, and a bit of California, detached from the mainland, will have drifted toward the Aleutian trench.

In summary, then, the question that puzzles scientists most is what creates the enormous stresses in the earth's crust?

Through much of seismic mythology two ideas recurred. The first of these was that something was imprisoned within the earth—a whale, a giant mole, a storm, or the monstrous children of Mother Earth. The second was that earthquakes had something to do with the sea; in Greek mythology, Poseidon, brother of Zeus and god of the sea, was also the "Earthshaker," and devoutly feared.

For many years, geophysicists have attempted to describe the actual counterparts of these mythical animals and storms. At the same time, they have tried to relate these unseeable subterranean forces to their trenches, the tearing of sea floors, the apparent drifting of continents, volcanic eruptions, and earthquakes.

Several decades ago, it was believed by scientists that the earth was cooling and as it shrank the crust was buckling and cracking. Today, however, most geologists and earthquake scientists believe exactly the opposite. They now contend that

---

*Scientists now believe that the Pacific is only 90 million years old, the youngest of the oceans.

the earth's interior is a roaring furnace, producing prodigious heat through the breakdown of radioactive elements such as uranium and thorium. Miners working as deep as two and three miles know well how hot rock walls can get, sometimes registering 160° F and more.

Tests have proven that heat increases steadily with depth and at the base of the crust may reach 1,500° F, the temperature of molten aluminum. Only enormous pressure keeps the mantle from becoming totally liquid.

Some geologists believed that this heat causes expansion of the earth, stretching the crust like a balloon. Or, as others suggested, it may be that temperatures and pressures cause abrupt molecular changes in the rock, just as these awesome forces change graphite into diamonds in the laboratory. Accompanying changes in volume could cause uplift or subsidence and a shifting of the crust.

Still another theory pictured the plastic material of the upper mantle seething in slow convection currents, somewhat like jam boiling on a stove. These currents, though infinitesimally slow, drag against the solid crystal rocks, in places pulling and torturing them until they rupture with a shocking release of power.

During the past few years, scientists throughout the world have come up with a striking new geological earth quake theory called "plate tectonics," which may contain the final truth. The theory offers a simple, yet comprehensive explanation for continental drift, mountain building and volcanism, all of which clarify the underlying cause of earth tremors. In brief, the theory holds that the surface of the earth consists of about ten giant, 50-mile thick plastic rock plates. Floating on the earth's semi-molten mantle and propelled by as yet undetermined forces, the plates are in constant motion. These great tectonic plates that carry oceans are moving about five times faster than the plates that are supporting continents. In relation to certain "hot spots" in the earth that appear to be stationary, oceanic plates move

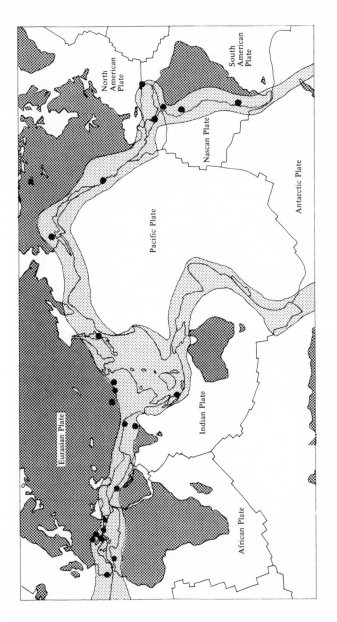

Plate Tectonics. The slow movement of the plates on the earth's crust are resisted by friction until stress builds up to the point where rock fractures, causing an earthquake. As shown on the plottings, *most of the earthquakes occur along the edges of these plates; the small-dot shaded area shows the earthquake-prone "belts" of the world.*

an average of four inches a year, whereas continental plates move only about three-fourths of an inch annually. Using all available data on plate motions from advanced computer techniques, scientists have been able to obtain motions of the ten major plates. Earthquake data and the orientation of large fracture zones observed on the ocean floors gave them local directions of plate motions. Data from the magnetic alignments of rocks along the ocean floors provided the velocity of the motions. Recent discoveries show that half of the Atlantic Ocean is on the same plate as North and South America, whereas the other half belongs to Europe. Also, it is interesting to note that some plates move faster than others, even though they don't relate to oceans or continents.

Each plate rotates around an imaginary axis that passes through the earth's center, but this does not necessarily coincide with the earth's rotational axis. To obtain a more accurate idea of the motions of the plates surrounding this great Pacific Plate, it at one point was considered stationary in order that the relative motions of its neighboring plates could be determined. The plate spans the entire Pacific Ocean and extends from Alaska to the South Seas.

The method makes it possible to predict the relative motions of different plates everywhere around their boundaries. These motions vary in different locations. In some places, such as along mid-oceanic ridges, plates are moving away from each other as molten rock rises to form new ocean floors. In other places, like along California's San Andreas fault, two plates are sliding horizontally past each other. In yet other areas, such as along the Japanese Trench, one plate is sliding under the edge of another.

The relative movement velocities between plates vary widely. Europe is moving away from North America at a rate of about three-quarters of an inch a year, while the East Pacific Rise at Easter Island spreads at the rate of some eight inches a year. Researchers are wondering whether these big plates are becoming deformed as they move.

The research has shown that the North and South American Plates don't behave as one plate, as had been supposed. Relative to South America, North America is moving westward about a quarter of an inch a year.

Baja California is cited as an excellent example of surface expression of plate movement. Baja, along with a slice of western California, belongs to the Pacific Plate. The rest of Mexico and much of California and the rest of the continental United States reside on the North American Plate. The Pacific Plate is moving at a rate of a little more than an inch a year in relation to the North American Plate. This movement caused Baja to break away from the Mexican mainland about five million years ago, and as a result the Gulf of California was formed. The gulf is widening about two inches per year.

Scientists aren't sure what the Gulf of California is going to do. Eventually, at its northern end it will open either toward the ocean or inland. There is no way to determine if the North American Plate is going to break in that area. Currently, the San Andreas fault is considered by most scientists to be the present plate boundary. But it is possible that in the future North America will break away somewhere else.

Recently, an intensive investigation of global tectonics was launched by the United States, Peru, and Chile. The investigation off the west coast of South America will test the hypothesis that much of the world's major resources of nonferrous ores are located in modern or suspected ancient zones where the giant plates converge. The plate borders are also generally recognized as earthquake zones.

Despite the widespread acceptance of global tectonics in the earth sciences, there is only limited knowledge regarding the complete cycle that takes place and of the degree to which these new tectonics theories can guide practical investigations of such geologic phenomena as minerals and petroleum location.

The investigation is a cooperative effort by the National

Oceanic and Atmospheric Administration of the U.S. Department of Commerce, the Hawaii Institute of Geophysics, Oregon State University, the Geophysical Institute of Peru, and the University of Chile's Department of Geophysics and Geodesy.

The investigation is centered on the Nazca Plate, which is bounded on the west by the East Pacific Rise, a 3,000 foot high underwater mountain range, and on the east by the Peru-Chile Trench, a deep chasm in the seabed off the South American coast. The water in the area under study is about 15,000 feet deep.

According to the global tectonics theory, the eastern edge of the Nazca Plate is moving into the earth along the Peru-Chile Trench. While this is going on, molten rock from the earth's interior is moving through the East Pacific Rise and forming new sea floor. The new material spreads away from the East Pacific Rise generally west toward the mid-Pacific and east toward South America. This spreading is one explanation for continental drift, the theory that as the plates move, they carry the continents with them.

One of the more interesting aspects of the investigation involves a detailed study of the ocean area near the location of the 1970 earthquake in Peru which took over 70,000 lives in the worst natural disaster in the history of the western hemisphere. This is the area where the Nazca Plate converges on the Peru-Chile Trench, one of the world's major earthquake zones.

The purpose of the investigation is to study in detail the processes of crustal formation and the destruction of the sea bed that takes place as it moves into the earth. The expedition will undertake geophysical, geochemical, and marine geological studies of the Nazca Plate's two edges and attempt to link these events and processes by geophysical studies of the structure and changes of the intervening plate.

* * *

In March of 1977, scientists mounting a major oceanographic expedition discovered an astounding wealth of wholly unexpected sea life and volcanic activity deep beneath the eastern Pacific where a new section of the earth's crust is apparently forming.

The Galapagos Rift Expedition sent its divers 9,000 feet by submarine into a huge crustal fracture zone. There, they discovered geysers of hot water pouring from giant fissures in fresh lava, sending long plumes of brine sparkling upward into the near-freezing lower levels of the sea. They also discovered fresh lava pouring out into the sea bottom, squeezed or erupting from the hot, semi-molten material of the deep earth's interior mantle beneath the crust.

To scientists, such findings mean a new theory about the deep ocean floor as well as the volcanic and earthquake activities which mark the formation of continents and the evolutions of the earth. According to Robert D. Ballard, the chief scientist for the expedition, and Tjeerd H. Van Andel, professor of geology at Stanford University, the latest discoveries will also revolutionize deep-sea biology.

With thirty scientists and three ships making up the expedition sponsored by the National Science Foundation, the target area was along a curious, broken valley 600 miles southwest of Panama between two large undersea mountain ranges running east and west for nearly 1,000 miles. This Galapagos Rift zone forms part of a huge global network of mid-ocean rifts and ridges, 40,000 miles long in all, where the earth's great crust is divided into great plates that float above an interior mantle of semi-liquid, molten rock. Some of these plates are far larger than the continents that ride on them, and the rift zone marks the boundary between the Cocos Plate to the north and the Nazca Plate to the south. Running at right angles to the Galapagos Rift is the East Pacific Rise which marks another plate boundary. West of that boundary is the great Pacific Plate, which stretches from California almost down to Antarctica.

Of course, earth scientists believe that these plate boundaries form dynamic "spreading centers" where the plastic materials of earth's interior mantle squeezes, or at times erupts violently upward to form new crust and to shove the plates apart. While grinding their way across the earth, the plates collide with other plates and many of them dip downward along the edges of the continents to rejoin the mantle below and melt within it. Thus, the trenches along the coastlines of the Americas, Japan, etc., are marked by violent earthquakes and volcanic eruptions.

The latest evidence suggests that the Galapagos Rift zone marks a significant "spreading center" where new crust is welling upward to form the brand-new lavas that scientists are observing. The basalts photographed and collected by this expedition are absolutely fresh, but as the ships move away from the center of the rift, the lava appears to grow older.

Scientists are seeing some of the very freshest material emerging from the earth's crust. One scientist said, "It was born only yesterday and some of it is literally being born this very minute . . . to drive the earth's great oceanic crustal plates into motion and keep the continents drifting imperceptibly across the globe."

Obtaining the relative motions of the plates gave researchers the opportunity to test the now famous Wilson-Morgan "hot spot" hypothesis. According to the theory by Drs. J. T. Wilson of Toronto and W. J. Morgan of Princeton, several chains of islands have been created by plates drifting over hot spots. These spots may be fixed with respect to each other or may represent locations of "plumes" of molten material rising from the molten outer core of the earth through the mantle. Examples of hot spot sites are Yellowstone National Park and Iceland.

If the hot spots are fixed, one can determine the motions over them which explain the island chains and are consistent with the relative motions of the plates. Wilson and Morgan have demonstrated that over the past ten million years, the hot spots stayed relatively fixed with respect to each other.

During that length of time the huge Pacific Plate appears to have moved northwesterly some 500 miles over a hot spot that is now under the Hawaiian Islands. Strings of volcanic islands extending northwesterly from Hawaii have been cited as part of the evidence that the hot spot was under them at various times in the past.

Where hot spots meet, friction sometimes temporarily locks them in place, causing stresses to build up near their edges. Eventually, it is that sudden release of pent-up energy that causes the violent trembling of the earth—as off the Eurasian Plate, causing the deep-seated quakes characteristic of the Japanese Archipelago. In California, along the San Andreas fault, two great plates are sliding past each other. The sliver west of the fault, which is located on the Pacific Plate, is moving toward the northwest. The rest of the state is resting on the North American Plate, which is moving westward. It was the sudden movement of a portion of the fault that had been locked in place for centuries that caused the great 1906 San Francisco earthquake.

The San Francisco Bay area is not the only main American seismic risk area. When quake centers are marked on a map of the world, it becomes clear that many earthquakes do indeed occur along plate boundaries. The earthquake belt marked "ring of fire" around the Pacific Ocean, for example, neatly outlines the Pacific Plate. But earthquakes can also occur well within a plate, possibly because the plate structure has been weakened in those places during periods of ancient volcanism. Charleston, South Carolina, for example, is more than 1,000 miles away from the edge of the North American Plate; yet it lies in a seismically active area. In 1886, a major quake killed 27 people. New Madrid, Missouri, near the middle of the plate, was the site of three huge quakes in 1811 and 1812. Wrote one eyewitness of the sparsely populated area: "The whole land was moved and moved like the waves of the sea. With the explosions and bursting of the ground, large fissures were formed, some of which closed immediately, while others were of varying widths, as much as 30 feet.'' This quake was felt from Canada to the Gulf of Mexico and from the Rocky Mountains to the Atlantic ocean.

Whichever of these actual mechanisms are triggered, earthquakes are intimately related to volcanoes. For example, four out of five of the world's shocks are recorded on the Pacific rim, named the "rim of fire" because of its many volcanic peaks. Alaska suffers especially because it lies within this earthquake belt, one of the earth's most unstable areas. Many active fault lines constantly threaten Alaska with tremors. Beat and compressed, these lines converge near Anchorage and their ominous pattern may well have triggered the March 27, 1964 earthquakes which tragically shook a 500-mile long coastal area with a force of a thousand hydrogen bombs. In this case, it was not the rock slippage itself which caused the extensive damage, but rather the vibration, sliding, and settling of loose glacial-alluvial deposits, that caused the damage. These deposits responded to shocks much as grains of sand dance on a board when it is struck violently.

During the course of a year there may be a thousand shocks which do a minimal amount of damage, and another 10,000 earthquakes which can be felt by human beings. But the more than 1,000 seismograph stations around the world may detect half a million tremors in a 12-month period of time.

This constant quivering of our restless planet, strange as it seems, has beneficial as well as destructive results. Seismic waves provide almost our sole means of studying the earth's deep interior.

But, more important, repeated uplifting of the earth's crust, with its various quakes, is essential to life as we know it. Mountains are constantly eroding; if they were not raised again, the world would become an awful place of stagnant seas and swamps. The seismic tremors which cause so much death and destruction are the inexorable ticks of our planetary clock, the pulse beats of earth. Were they to stop, ours would indeed become a dead world.

Earthquakes and Their Faults

In brief, the earthquake is known to humans directly as a trembling or shaking of the ground. Commonly, earthquakes are barely perceptible to the senses, but sometimes so violent as to crack or collapse strong buildings, break water and gas mains, cause gaping cracks in the ground, and bring great loss of life and property.

To better understand the nature of the earthquake waves, or seismic waves, scientists study and interpret the records of the seismograph, a sensitive instrument that can record earthquakes thousands of miles away. A seismograph can detect small vibrations that could not be recognized by the human sense. The records of seismic waves that have passed through the earth's interior regions provide the evidence scientists seek.

The vast majority of important earthquakes that can be analyzed at long distances from their sources are produced by a type of movement in the earth's crust known as faulting. This phenomenon is simply a sudden slippage between two rock masses separated by a fracture surface. Small-scale demonstrations of faulting can be seen in common materials such as dry soil, concrete, or rock, which easily fracture when compressed or when the underlying support is removed—for example, cracks in pavements, sidewalks, or masonry walls. At first the material withstands the forces that tend to bend or twist it, but when the limit of strength is reached the material suddenly cracks, releasing the strain by a mass displacement in which the mass on one side slips past the other.

Highly indurated rocks of the earth's outermost layers are both strong and brittle, as reflected by the various kinds of materials we see all about us. Under great deforming stress* rock actually bends elastically like steel, but in an amount scarcely detectable in small masses. Despite its ability to withstand great stress with only slight bending, or strain, a given rock has an elastic limit. If it is strained beyond this limit, a fracture occurs and the bent rock snaps suddenly back to its normal shape.

An earthquake is the reaction set off by the sudden release of elastic strain. As in a bow slowly bent, the rocks have gradually accumulated energy, only to release it with great suddenness. In brief, there are certain mountain-making belts of the earth's outer layers in which faulting occurs repeatedly as enormous masses of rock are pushed past one another, or over one another, generating countless shocks.

A simple model of a mechanism of earthquakes can be constructed with a strip of tempered steel, such as a coping saw blade, whose ends are tightly clamped in wooden blocks. If the blocks are forced to move parallel with one another in opposite directions to produce an S-bend in the blade, the blade can be bent slowly to the breaking point. When the blade snaps, the broken ends whip back into straight pieces, but the ends are now considerably offset. The twang of the break is equivalent to the earth tremor. This model illustrates the so-called "elastic-rebound" theory of earthquake origin. The theory was proven beyond doubt as the explanation for major earthquakes by actual measurements of the bending of the ground on either side of a known line of faulting both before and after the great San Francisco earthquake of 1906. Two scientists from the University of California in Berkeley rechecked by precise geodetic surveying methods the exact positions of several triangulation stations on mountain peaks on both sides of the San Andreas fault that runs through San Francisco and on which the slip had taken place. They found

---

*Stress is strictly defined as force per unit of surface area. The two words *force* and *stress* can usually be used interchangeably in the various writing without regard to a strict difference in meaning.

that after the earthquake, the ground lying close to the fault had moved most with a gradually decreasing amount of ground movement as the distance from the fault increased. The maximum measured displacement along the fault was 21 feet.

The slow bending was accumulating stored energy for hundreds of years before the earthquake occurred, and the rocks were already bent almost to their elastic limit when the first triangulation surveys were made. Slow bending was still in progress between 1850 and 1906. Then on the frightful April morning in 1906, the rock suddenly snapped to a new position, releasing a tremendous quantity of energy in a series of seismic waves. These spread rapidly away from the fault line, dying out gradually with increasing distance.

Faults of the type which produced the San Francisco earthquake involve a geometry of displacement in which most of the motion of one block with respect to the other is in the horizontal direction. Such a fault is known as a trans-current fault, or strike-slip fault.* These kinds of faults are well-represented throughout California where they form the dominant geologic elements. Longest and best known is the San Andreas fault, nearly 600 miles long which can be traced from the Salton Basin, along the foot of the San Bernardino Mountain range of southern California, northward continuously to the San Francisco Bay region, where the fault passes into the Pacific Ocean. Movement occurs locally from time to time along the transcurrent faults of California, generating earthquakes of greatly varying intensities. The horizontal movement along these fault lines is strikingly illustrated by the displacement of such linear features as roads, fences, pipe lines, and orchard rows.

A major strike-slip fault, such as the San Andreas fault, produces a conspicuous rift zone which in certain places is a straight trench occupied by small lakes or stream segments.

---

*A transcurrent, or strike-slip, fault displays horizontal movement, the sides moving in opposite directions.

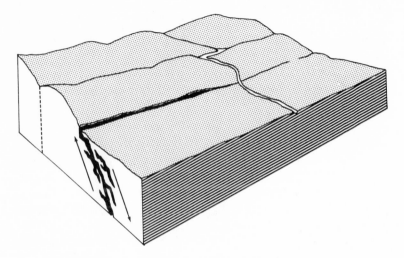

Dip-Slip Fault. Characterized by vertical or oblique movement in opposing directions.

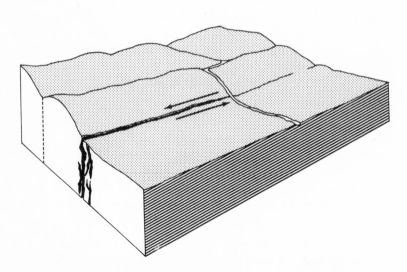

Strike-Slip Fault. Characterized by lateral movement in opposing directions.

Where a stream has flowed across the fault line for a long period of time during which repeated movements have occurred, the stream may show a marked offset where it has turned to follow the rift for a short distance in order to maintain flow to the displaced downstream portion of its channel. Where a strike-slip fault cuts across hilly or mountainous terrain, imposing fault scarps (known as abrupt steps) may result, because the two parts of a mountain mass are moved past one another, exposing the fault plane.

Finally, it should be noted that the seismic (earthquake) waves felt as shaking, vary in character in different earth materials. Hard crystalline rock such as granite exhibits greater short-period (rapid) motion while deep valley alluviums exhibit greater long-period (slow) motion which is more likely to damage structures; the bulk of earthquake damage occurs to structures on thick alluvial deposits, possibly because more structures are built on valley floors. Other hazardous settings involve unstable soils that may settle differentially or fail by cracking or, if water-saturated, by liquefaction and lateral flow on gentle slopes, or landsliding on steep slopes.

Perhaps one of the most interesting of earthquakes to occur in recent times was the one which occurred in Fukui, Japan, in 1948. While no surface faulting was observed during this quake, some important data was obtained. The magnitude was 7.3. In the area which included most of an alluviated plain, over 75 percent of the structures were demolished. Over 5,000 people were killed, with nearly 1,000 in the city of Fukui alone.

What was unusual about this tragedy was the large number of fissures of secondary character which opened up in the alluvium. To quote an official report:

> A tragic event frequently described in fiction but rarely occurring in actuality was verified. The party learned of the fact that a young woman had been crushed to death in a fissure in the near neighborhood. The site was visited

and the witnesses interviewed. The victim, Mrs. Sadako Nankyo, 37, was working in a rice paddy, located close by the house at 33 Shissaku-machi, Fukui City, when the shocks were felt. She started out of the paddy but fell into a fissure which, it was said, opened to about 4 feet in width. It closed upon her to the chin, instantly crushing her to death. The body was immediately dug out of the ground (only a faint remainder of the course of the fissure could be traced) by neighbors and the woman's husband. Seven people saw the woman in the ground after the quake and several of them were eye-witnesses of the happening.

This is the only such documented case of its kind in recorded history except for that of the cow in the 1906 San Francisco earthquake. Actually there is nothing incredible in the account. From the nature of fissuring and cracking described in many earthquakes, such accidents must occasionally happen. Recorded history contains many vague and doubtful or incomplete references to such instances. In Japan, as in other countries, the exaggerated fear of being "swallowed up" during an earthquake is widespread. The risk, though real, is much less than that of many other earthquake dangers.*

Earthquake Energy

Interpretation of seismograms has made possible a calculation of the quantities of energy released as wave motion by earthquakes of various magnitudes. It was in 1935 that the world's leading seismologist, Charles F. Richter, brought forth the scale of earthquake magnitudes describing the quantity of energy released at the earthquake focus.

The Richter Scale consists of numbers ranging from 0 to 8.6. The scale is logarithmic which is to say that the energy of the shock increases by powers of ten in relation to Richter magnitude numbers.

*Every increase of one number on the Richter scale, say from magnitude 5.5 to magnitude 6.5 means the ground motion is 10 times greater.

Recently this 42-year-old scale has been revised, changing the numerical ratings of some earlier disastrous earthquakes. For example, San Francisco's 1906 quake is being downgraded. According to a new version on the Richter scale, that temblor will be officially listed as measuring 7.9 instead of 8.25. And the 1960 quake in Chile released 62 times as much energy as previously thought. The tragic Alaskan earthquake in 1964 which had been pegged at 8.4 will now be upgraded to 9.2. Many seismologists disagree with the revisions, saying that all such arbitrary measurements have been and will always be in question.

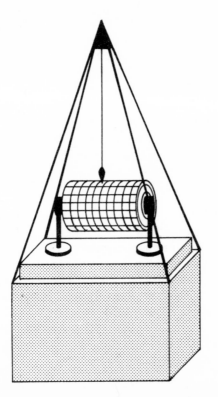

Seismograph. Basically composed of a pendulum or magnet attached to a fixed source. A recording stylus is attached to the pendulum/magnet to record its movement on a calibrated drum.

Yet, these new magnitude readings were developed by Hiroo Kanamori, a seismologist at the California Institute of Technology, as a result of his studies into the relationship between earthquake shock waves and the numbers used by Richter. According to the young scientist, the 1906 quake in San Francisco developed from a break in the San Andreas fault which was less than 200 miles long, although the fault line is more than 600 miles in length.

For breaks in a fault this short, the current Richter scale

Magnitude	Richter Scale
0	Although earthquakes can be detected with magnitudes of -1, -2, -3, etc., this figure generally is given for exceedingly small shocks. Energy release is 6.3×10^5 ergs.
2.5-3	Quake can be felt if it is nearby. About 100,000 shallow quakes of this magnitude occur per year.
4.5	Can cause local damage.
5	Energy release about equal to first atomic bomb, Alamogordo, New Mexico, 1945.
6	Destructive in a limited area. About 100 shallow quakes per year of this magnitude.
7	Rated a major earthquake above this magnitude. Quake can be recorded over whole earth. About 14 per year this great or greater.
7.8	San Francisco quake of 1906, often cited as 8.3. Energy release 3.3×10^{24} ergs.
8.4	Close to maximum known. Energy release 2×10^{25} ergs. Examples: Honshu 1933, Assam 1950, Alaska 1964.
8.6	Maximum observed between 1900 and 1950. Three million times as much energy released as in first atomic bomb.

Total annual energy release by earthquake is roughly on the order of 10×10^{26} ergs, most of it being from a very few quakes of magnitude greater than 7.

tends to over-estimate the amount of energy released during a shock. For longer breaks, however, the scale underestimates a temblor's magnitude significantly. Richter's scale was really based on the measurement of earthquake waves stretching less than 100 miles from crest to crest, while the new scale makes use of seismic waves of 300 miles or more. Instruments capable of measuring these very long seismic wavelengths have been developed during the past 20 years. Only now are seismologists learning to interpret the measurements accurately. Certainly, Richter's old scale remains accurate for small and moderate quakes up to magnitudes of 7 or 7.5. But for the first time, the largest temblors knows as "great quakes" will be recorded above 8.9.

Thus, the new system will not replace the Richter scale, but will change how the higher magnitudes are computed. At the same time, Dr. Paul C. Jennings, California Institute of Technology professor of applied mechanics, struck an optimistic note about the effects of the so-called "great quakes." He said, "These great seismic events are not uniformly associated with catastrophic damage."

Earthquake Effects

The actual destructiveness of an earthquake also depends upon factors other than the energy release given by Richter magnitude—for example, closeness to the epicenter (the surface point directly above the focus of the earthquake) and nature of the subsurface earth materials. Intensity scales, designed to measure observed earth-shaking effects, are important in engineering aspects of seismology.

An intensity scale used extensively in the United States is the modified Mercalli scale as prepared by Richter in 1956. Previously, the Ross-Forel intensity scale was in use in this country and remains in use in other parts of the world. The modified Mercalli scale of 1956 recognizes 12 levels of inten-

The seismograph is the principal instrument of seismology which detects and records earth movements caused by passing vibrations. Sensors called seismometers use the principle of inertia to measure the relative motion between a free mass (which tends to remain at rest) and a pier-mounted frame (which moves with the earth). Ideally, seismometers are mounted on rock-imbedded concrete piers in quiet locations; in practice, the instruments must tune out the persistent clatter of civilization, or record a minor "earthquake" every time a truck goes by.

This motion, amplified and transmitted as an electrical impulse, provides the familiar "signature" of the seismogram. To obtain a full description of earth movement, three components of motion—vertical, east-west, and north-south—must be sensed and recorded on three sets of instruments. Also, sensors which respond to various seismic wavelengths must be employed.

sity, designated by Roman numerals I through XII. Each intensity is described in terms of phenomena that any person might experience. For example, at intensity IV hanging objects swing, a vibration like that of a passing truck is felt, standing automobiles rock, and windows and dishes rattle. Damage to various classes of masonry is used to establish criteria in the higher numbers of the scale. At an intensity of XII, damage to manmade structures is nearly total and large masses of rock are displaced.

Many of the destructive effects of a severe earthquake are secondary, in the sense that the earthquake movements set off gravity movements of bodies of rock, soil and alluvial overburden. An example is the Good Friday earthquake of March 27, 1964, centered about 75 miles from the city of Anchorage, Alaska. Magnitude on the Richter scale was 8.4 to 8.6, which is close to the maximum known. Intensity on the Mercalli scale was probably VII to VIII in Anchorage, but, as most buildings were frame construction, damage was largely through secondary effects. Of these, the most important were landslides of great masses of gravel overlying layers of unstable clay. Major snowslides were set off in the adjacent mountains.

Throughout the region of the Alaskan earthquake, sudden drops or uplifts in land level took place at points as far distant as 300 miles from the epicenter and covered a total area of about 80,000 square miles. A belt of uplift reaching a maximum of 30 feet runs parallel with the coast and largely offshore, while a broad zone of shallow subsidence, reaching depths somewhat greater than -6 feet lies along the landward side of the uplift zone. The epicenter lay between these zones. Sudden rise of the sea floor produced a train of seismic sea waves.

The supposed fault along which slippage occurred to generate the Alaska earthquake is not exposed on land, but presumably lies at depth in the offshore zone in a position between the zone of subsidence and the zone of uplift. The entire zone of seismic activity occupies a position between the Aleutian volcanic arc on the northwest and the deep submarine Aleutian trench on the southeast.

THE MERCALLI INTENSITY SCALE
(As modified by Charles F. Richter in 1956 and rearranged)

If most of these effects are observed	*then the intensity is:*
Earthquake shaking not felt. But people may observe marginal effects of large distance earthquakes without identifying these effects as earthquake-caused. Among them: trees, structures, liquids, bodies of water sway slowly, or doors swing slowly.	*I*
Effect on people: Shaking felt by those at rest, especially if they are indoors, and by those on upper floors.	*II*
Effect on people: Felt by most people indoors. Some can estimate duration of shaking. But many may not recognize shaking of buildings as caused by an earthquake: the shaking is like that caused by the passing of light trucks.	*III*
Other effects: Hanging objects swing. *Structural effects:* Windows or doors rattle. Wooden walls and frames creak.	*IV*
Effect on people: Felt by everyone indoors. Many estimate duration of shaking. But they still may not recognize it as caused by an earthquake. The shaking is like that caused by the passing of heavy trucks, though sometimes, instead, people may feel the sensation of a jolt, as if a heavy ball had struck the walls. *Other effects:* Hanging objects swing. Standing autos rock. Crockery clashes, dishes rattle or glasses clink. *Structural effects:* Doors close, open or swing. Windows rattle.	*V*

Effect on people: Felt by everyone indoors and by most people outdoors. Many now estimate not only the duration of shaking but also its direction and have no doubt as to its cause. Sleepers wakened.

Other effects: Hanging objects swing. Shutters or pictures move. Pendulum clocks stop, start or change rate. Standing autos rock. Crockery clashes, dishes rattle or glasses clink. Liquids disturbed, some spilled. Small unstable objects displaced or upset.

Structural effects: Weak plaster and Masonry D* crack. Windows break. Doors close, open or swing.

VI

Effect on people: Felt by everyone. Many are frightened and run outdoors. People walk unsteadily.

Other effects: Small church or school bells ring. Pictures thrown off walls, knicknacks and books off shelves. Dishes or glasses broken. Furniture moved or overturned. Trees, bushes shaken visibly, or heard to rustle.

Structural effects: Masonry D* damaged; some cracks in Masonry C*. Weak chimneys break at roof line. Plaster, loose bricks, stones, tiles, cornices, unbraced parapets and architectural ornaments fall. Concrete irrigation ditches damaged.

VII

Effect on people: Difficult to stand. Shaking noticed by auto drivers.

Other effects: Waves on ponds; water turbid with mud. Small slides and caving in along sand or gravel banks. Large bells ring. Furniture broken. Hanging objects quiver.

Structural effects: Masonry D* heavily damaged: Masonry C* damaged, partially collapses in some

VIII

---

*Masonry A: Good workmanship and mortar, reinforced, designed to resist lateral forces.

Masonry B: Good workmanship and mortar, reinforced.

Masonry C: Good workmanship and mortar, unreinforced.

Masonry D: Poor workmanship and mortar and weak materials, like adobe.

cases; some damage to Masonry B*; none to Masonry A*. Stucco and some masonry walls fall. Chimneys, factory stacks, monuments, towers, elevated tanks twist or fall. Frame houses moved on foundations if not bolted down; loose panel walls thrown out. Decayed piling broken off.

Effect on people: General fright. People thrown to ground.

Other effects: Changes in flow or temperature of springs and wells. Cracks in wet ground and on steep slopes. Steering of autos affected. Branches broken from trees.

Structural effects: Masonry D* destroyed; Masonry C* heavily damaged, sometimes with complete collapse; Masonry B* is seriously damaged. General damage to foundations. Frame structures, if not bolted, shifted off foundations. Frames racked. Reservoirs seriously damaged. Underground pipes broken.

IX

Effect on people: General Panic.

Other effects: Conspicuous cracks in ground. In areas of soft ground, sand is ejected through holes and piles up into a small crater, and, in muddy areas, water fountains are formed.

Structural effects: Most masonry and frame structures destroyed along with their foundations. Some well-built wooden structures and bridges destroyed. Serious damage to dams, dikes and embankments. Railroads bent slightly.

X

Effect on people: General panic.

Other effects: Large landslides. Water thrown on banks of canals, rivers, lakes, etc. Sand and mud shifted horizontally on beaches and flat land.

Structural effects: General destruction of buildings. Underground pipelines completely out of service. Railroads bent greatly.

XI

Effect on people: General panic.
Other effects: Same as for Intensity X
Structural effects: Damage nearly total, the ultimate catastrophe.
Other effects: Large rock masses displaced. Lines of sight and level distorted. Objects thrown into air.

XII

APPROXIMATE RELATIONSHIPS

MAGNITUDE	EXPECTED ANNUAL INCIDENCE[1]	FELT AREA (SQ. MI.)	DISTANCE FELT (ST. MI.)[2]	INTENSITY (MAXIMUM EXPECTED MODIFIED MERCALLI)[3]
3.0-3.9	49,000	750	15	II-III
4.0-4.9	6,200	3,000	30	IV-V
		1 thousand tons[3] of TNT 4.2×10^{19} ergs		
5.0-5.9	800	15,000	70	VI-VII
6.0-6.9	120	50,000	125	VII-VIII
		1 million tons[3] of TNT 4.2×10^{22} ergs		
7.0-7.0	18	200,000	250	IX-X
8.0-8.9	1	800,000	450	XI-XII

[1] B. Gutenberg and C. F. Richter, *Seismicity of the Earth and Associated Phenomena,* Princeton University Press, Princeton, N. J., 1954, page 18.

[2] H. Benioff and B. Gutenberg, "General Introduction to Seismology," *Earthquakes in Kern County During 1952,* State of California, Division of Mines, Bulletin 171, San Francisco, 1955, page 133.

[3] U.S. Department of Defense, *Effects of Nuclear Weapons,* S. Glasstone, *Ed.;* Government Printing Office, Washington, D. C., 1962, page 14.

V

Predicting and Planning for Inevitable Earthquakes

Earthquakes prediction is a rapidly developing technology. And, because of this, it is an emerging science with successes and failures, as well as some total surprises. Most seismologists agree that although it may be one or two decades before a proven system is available, serious predictions can now be issued. The goal of such a prediction effort is to predict damaging earthquakes sufficiently far in advance and with sufficient accuracy that the prediction will result in a significant reduction in loss of life and property. A secondary but closely related goal includes predicting the effects of an earthquake in order to guide rationally the loss-saving actions between the prediction and the occurrence of the earthquake.

There are three basic aspects to earthquake prediction:
1) Location of the areas where large earthquakes are most likely to occur;
2) Observation within these areas of measurable changes (earthquake precursors) and determination of the area and time over which the earthquake will occur;
3) Development of models of the earthquake source in order to reliably interpret the precursors.

Deprived of its ancient mythology, the mystery and strength of the earthquake is slowly being diminished, analyzed like a simple biological or geological specimen. Suppose respected scientific voices, armed with data from instruments that gave the earth's silent strain and creep and tilt, were able to warn the Manhattan populace hours, even minutes, before a quake? How many thousands might escape collapsing buildings, roofs, falling walls? Everyone agrees that an effective earthquake warning system would be of incalculable value to man.

The shock waves from stunned and smashed disaster areas reverberating around the world are demanding to know whether man can somehow see what is going on inside our tortured planet and know when the earth we so trustingly build our houses upon will shift and shudder.

In China, for example, over 10,000 scientists are studying how to predict earthquakes. In the United States, there are only 200 doing such work. The Chinese programs have already saved thousands of lives. Our programs thus far have saved none.

However, American earthquake scientists are busy at work correcting this. Today, these scientists are moving ever closer to reliable earthquake forecasts. In California, for example, U.S. Geological Survey scientists predicted that an earthquake measuring 3.5 on the Richter scale would occur within a 15 kilometer (9.4 mile) radius of the Guido Canzoni ranch near Hollister during early January in 1977. On January 6, a shock measuring 3.2 rattled the buildings 10 kilometers (6.3 miles) from Hollister. This unpublicized prediction had been posted on one of the bulletin boards of the U.S. Geological Survey in Menlo Park on December 30, seven days before. It was just another example of successfully predicting small California temblors along the San Andreas fault system.

Is it possible that an earthquake with the magnitude of the one which hit New Madrid, Missouri, will ever be successfully predicted?

Scientists say yes.

Apparently it is becoming common to successfully fore-cast earthquakes along the seismically active San Andreas fault. But what about predicting earthquakes along less active faults?

Scientists Charles G. Bufe, Philip W. Harsh, and Robert D. Burford of the U.S. Geological Survey's Office of Earthquake Studies in Menlo Park made a major break-through in October of 1976 when they forecast a quake with a magnitude of 3 to 4 on the Richter scale within 6 weeks on an inactive fault line. The location they spotted was within a section of hilly terrain about four miles wide and five miles long near the Calaveras fault, not far from Mt. Hamilton. On December 8th, the earthquake struck about 10 miles east of San Jose and registered 3.2 on the Richter scale. The epicenter was just 4.2 miles south of Mt. Hamilton's Lick Observatory, on the flanks of the San Felipe hills.

The three scientists had announced in their forecast they were 95 percent confident of their prediction's accuracy. The statistical probability of a quake occurring within 24 days of any randomly selected date is only about 10 percent. "Our forecast," they said, "is unusually significant. It reflects progress is being made in research aimed at developing an earthquake prediction capability."

But predicting how people will react to public forecasts is still somewhat of an inexact science.

In an effort to discover what reactions there would be following the forecast of a major earthquake, J. Eugene Haas and Dennis S. Mileti of the University of Colorado's Institute of Behavioral Science interviewed thousands of public officials, businessmen, journalists, and families in earthquake-prone areas of California. Their frightening con-clusion was that unless planning is begun now to prevent it, the first credible earthquake prediction for a city the size of Manhattan, Los Angeles, or San Francisco will exact a very high price in economic dislocation and social disruption.

In their detailed study, Haas and Mileti developed the

following four-phase scenario which in their opinion, based upon all their interviews, will occur:

• In January of 1977, experts announced there is a 25 percent probability that a damaging earthquake will occur within three years in a major urban area. About a fifth of the affected homeowners try to buy earthquake insurance for the first time.

• Refining their information based upon new data, the experts predict that in August 1978 there is a 50 percent probability of a 7-size Richter scale quake occurring in the fall of 1980. Suddenly, new earthquake insurance policies become unavailable in "target" areas. Construction projects are held up and unemployment in the building trades approaches 80 percent. People cut back on spending and place more money into savings accounts. Many citizens consider moving out of the area. By the fall, 10 percent have done so.

• In November of 1979, the scientists cite an 80 percent probability of a 7.2 to 7.6 quake during September 1980. People begin stockpiling food and medical supplies. The remaining residents make plans to leave, and both retail sales and real estate values drop precipitously, while unemployment continues to climb.

• In June 1980, the earthquake is pinpointed to occur during the first week of September. By the end of August, some 60 percent of the area's residents have left, 10 percent permanently. Of those remaining, many have begun eating and sleeping out and avoiding older, taller buildings. School openings are postponed. A week before the quake is due, government agencies move trailers and other temporary facilities, well away from buildings and power lines.

Haas and Mileti acknowledge that these preparations will have tremendous social costs. But the benefits in lives saved will be far greater, especially if such prediction were able to warn Manhattanites of a major earthquake. For example, despite their elaborate early-warning system, Chinese scientists missed the signs which heralded the 1976 8.2 magnitude quake in Hupeh Province. No prediction or evacuation orders were issued, and the quake caught large houses and other structures, killing some 655,000 people.

The Art of Predicting Earthquakes

Today, most research in earthquake prediction is aimed at measuring a wide variety of physical phenomena that may change prior to earthquakes. Over two hundred cases of such precursors have been reported primarily in the Soviet Union, Japan, China, and the U.S. Measurements of earthquake precursors can be grouped into five categories: stress changes, strain changes, effects of strain changes, changes in seismic measurements, and other changes.

Measurements of the levels or changes in stress could potentially be among the most important earthquake precursors, but no reliable technique is yet available even though several are under development.

Measurements of strain changes, however, have been widespread. Uplift and subsidence of areas of thousands of square kilometers by amounts of several centimeters have been detected using standard precise leveling techniques. Such uplifts can be related to the mean sea level using tide gauges, and in some cases, apparent local changes in sea level have been observed prior to earthquakes. Vertical motion is also detectable using gravimeters sensitive to microgal changes in the force of gravity. Precise triangulation and trilateration techniques allow mapping of horizontal strain changes over areas a few to tens of kilometers long. New methods being developed, such as using laser ranging to satellites or to the moon, or using radio signals from distant quasars, offer the possibility of measuring strain changes over distances of hundreds to thousands of kilometers. These techniques, particularly when refined to the ultimately expected precision of a few centimeters, offer a unique chance to measure plate motion and strain within the plates.

Strain can also be measured over distances of meters to a kilometer using strain meters, small trilateration networks, and tiltmeters. Over seventy meters that measure small tilts of the ground surface have been installed in California.

Strain associated with the tidal pull of the moon or other planets can be measured using microgal gravimeters and strain meters. Many earthquake predictions issued by persons not in the mainstream of scientific research are based on alignment of planets. While it is conceivable that such small forces could trigger earthquakes, there is no clear correlation between these forces and damaging earthquakes.

Many precursory changes have been noted that are believed to result from strain in the region of impending earthquakes. These range from changes in electrical conductivity and generation of electrical potential in the ground, to changes in the magnetic field and atmospheric electric fields, to changes in the quality or level of ground water, to changes in the emission of various gases, such as radon, in well water or in the soil.

Another class of earthquake precursor is changes in seismic measurements. Although these changes may be the results of stress or strain changes, it is more informative to group them separately because each depends on the measurement of seismic waves from local or distant earthquakes at one or more, typically a few to dozens or even hundreds, of seismic stations. These precursors range from changes in the distribution of earthquakes in location, time, or depth, to changes in the ratio of numbers of large earthquakes to small events, to changes in signal amplitude or frequency content, to changes in the velocity of these seismic waves. Velocity changes have been used to predict several small earthquakes but in many other cases, detailed studies have failed to measure precursory velocity changes. In some cases foreshocks have been observed to increase and then decrease prior to large earthquakes but many earthquakes are not preceded by foreshocks.

The fifth type of earthquake precursor is those that do not readily fit into the previous four categories. For example, hundreds of reports over many centuries have been made of unusual behavior of animals prior to earthquakes.

Other precursors may exist that have not been considered so far. It is important to keep an open mind on all conceivable phenomena in which change might be observed prior to earthquakes.

Seismologists have recently shown that the time between the onset of a precursory anomaly and the ensuing earthquake is, in most cases, related systematically to the magnitude of the earthquake. In the remaining cases the precursors occurred just prior to the event, irrespective of magnitude. Thus the first direct evidence of a magnitude 5 earthquake might be noticed months in advance and perhaps decades in advance of a magnitude 8 event. There is a relative lack of short-term precursors which is a prime reason why observations of abnormal animal behavior are being considered more seriously now.

In summary, the key to accurate predictions of earthquakes lies in observing and correctly interpreting precursors. A wide variety of such precursors have been observed and in a few cases used to predict events. Most of these precursors have been observed on only one instrument for a particular earthquake and many of the signals are close to the noise level for these instruments. No one precursor is known to occur before every type of earthquake. Thus at this point it is assumed that observations of a variety of precursors will be required to predict earthquakes reliably. Observations of a given precursor on many instruments of the same type are critically needed to show the size of the area over which the

Graphic recorders of data from tiltmeters, strain-meters, and magnetometers.

anomalies occur. As mentioned, the larger the earthquake, the larger the area over which stress is released and probably the larger the area over which precursors will be observed.

In short, the Age of Prediction is here. Some accurate predictions have been issued as well as some false alarms. Nevertheless, a credible prediction could be issued at any moment and the time is here and now to prepare to respond to such a prediction. Unlike many sciences, earthquake prediction cannot be developed in some laboratory and suddenly unveiled as a proven method. Evidence could be observed at any moment that may save people's lives and thus can not be withheld. Scientists in the field realize that they must provide such evidence immediately, with a responsible interpretation, to the public. They also realize that there is a finite chance of issuing a false alarm. Furthermore it is clear that a credible earthquake prediction could, in the worst case, cause more social and economic disruption than the ensuing earthquake. Earthquake prediction is an emerging technological advancement that offers the possibility to save many lives and significantly reduce economic losses if scientists, civic leaders, policy makers, and all citizens are prepared to respond properly.

* * *

Two billion people live in the world's seismic zones. Very few of them realize that a series of little-noticed events and discoveries are leading scientists closer to saving their lives: achieving a critical breakthrough in the ability to predict and possibly control earthquakes. A Buck Rogers concept? Hardly. Although earthquake science is the youngest observational science, longtime students of natural disasters have realized for some time that reliable earthquake forecasts are nearly at hand. In fact, the batting average for America's more frequent magnitude (3 on the Richter) tremors is running about .600* Obviously not good enough, scientists are nonetheless delighted since it indicates progress. Most important of all, geologists are detecting all the anomalies and precursors before every quake. Nothing is slipping through their networks.

But how will scientists predict the big ones, the colossal hammerings that rend the earth for hundreds of miles and send mountains crashing down? It appears that forecasting these poses problems of proportionate magnitude.

Geophysicist Amos Nur reminds us that "We are working with a global event. An earthquake shakes the entire planet. To fathom these, we must go beneath the surface symptoms and explain the inner workings of the earth in terms of physical processes, just as Newton's laws explained the external motions of the planet."

Long before the plate tectonics theory was conceived, scientists were aware that rocks fracture only under extreme stress. As early as 1910, geologist Harry Reid of Johns Hopkins University suggested that it should be possible to tell when and where quakes were likely to occur by keeping close tab on the buildup of stresses along a fault. But the knowledge, instruments and funds necessary to monitor many miles of fault line and interpret any findings simply did not

---

*This does not necessarily imply a 60 percent prediction capability; several have indeed been successfully predicted, but most have not been.

exist. Earthquake prediction did not draw much attention until 1949 when a devastating quake struck the Garm region of central Asia, causing an avalanche that buried the village of Khait and killed over 12,000 people. Stunned by the disaster, the Soviets organized a scientific expedition and sent it into the quake-prone area. Its mission was to discover any geologic changes—in effect, early warning signals—that might occur before future quakes. The expedition remained in central Asia for longer than anyone had expected. But it was time well spent. In 1971, at an international scientific meeting in Moscow, the Soviet scientists announced that they had significantly progressed toward their goal; they had learned how to recognize some signs of impending quakes.

The most important signal, they said was a change in the velocity of vibrations that pass through the earth's crust as a result of such disturbances as quakes, mining blasts or underground nuclear tests. In short, it was a discovery of wave-speed changes in relation to the behavior of rocks deep underground. Earth scientists have long known that tremors spread outward in two different types of seismic waves. One type of waves, P waves, cause any rock in their path to compress and then expand in the same direction as the waves are traveling. S waves move the rock in a direction that is perpendicular to their path. Because P waves travel faster than S waves, they reach seismographs first. The Russian scientists found that the difference in the arrival times of P and S waves began to decrease markedly for days, weeks, and even months before a quake. Then, shortly before the quake struck, the lead time mysteriously returned to normal. The Russians also learned that the longer the period of abnormal wave velocity before a quake, the larger the eventual tremor was likely to be.*

The implication of that information was not lost on vis-

---

*U.S. scientists now estimate that the change can occur as long as 25 to 75 years before a magnitude 8 quake, 6 to 10 years before a 7-pointer and 1 to 2 years before a magnitude of 6.

iting Westerners. As soon as he returned home from Moscow, Lynn Sykes, head of the seismology group of Columbia University's Lamont-Doherty Geological Observatory, urged one of his students, a young Indian doctoral candidate named Yash Aggarwal, to look for similar velocity shifts in records from Lamont-Doherty's network of seismographs in the Blue Mountain Lake region of the Adirondacks, in upper New York State, where tiny tremors occur frequently.

As it happens, a swarm of small earthquakes had taken place at approximately the time of the Moscow meeting. Aggarwal's subsequent analysis bore out the Russian claims: before each quake there had been a distinct drop in the lead time of the P waves. As significant as those changes seemed, U.S. seismologists felt that the information could not be really dependable as a quake-prediction signal without a more fundamental understanding of what was causing them. The explanation was already available. In the late 1960s, while studying the reaction of materials to great mechanical strains, a team of researchers under M.I.T. geologist William Brace had discovered that as a rock approaches its breaking point, there are unexpected changes in its properties. For one thing, its resistance to electricity increases; for another, the seismic waves passing through it slow down.

Both effects seemed related to a phenomenon called *dilatancy*—the opening of a myriad of tiny, often microscopic cracks in rock subjected to great pressure. Brace even suggested at the time that the physical changes associated with dilatancy might provide warning of an impending earthquake, but neither he nor anyone else was quite sure how to proceed with his proposal. Dilatancy was, in effect, put on the shelf.

The Russian discoveries reawakened interest in the subject. Geophysicist Christopher Scholz of Lamont-Doherty and Amos Nur at Stanford, both of whom had studied under Brace at M.I.T., independently published papers that used dilatancy to explain the Russian findings. Both reports pointed out an apparent paradox: when the cracks first open in the crustal rock its strength increases. Temporarily, the rock resists fracturing and the quake is delayed. At the same time, seismic waves slow down because they do not travel as fast through solid rock. Eventually ground water begins to seep into the new openings in the dilated rock, which causes the seismic-wave velocity to quickly return to normal. The water also has another effect: it weakens the rock until it suddenly gives way, causing the quake.

Soon California Institute of Technology's James Whitcomb, Ian Garmany, and Don Anderson weighed in with more evidence. In a search of past records, before the 1971 San Fernando quake (65 deaths), the largest in California in recent years, they discovered the P waves had returned to their normal velocity a few months before the tremor. Besides providing what amounted to a retroactive prediction of that powerful quake, the Caltech researchers demonstrated that it was primarily the velocity of the P waves, not the S waves that changed. Their figures were significant for another reason: the P wave velocity change was not caused by a quirk of geology in the Garm region or even in the Adirondacks, but was apparently a common symptom of the buildup of dangerous stresses in the earth.

In fact, dilatancy seems to explain virtually all the strange effects observed prior to earthquakes. As cracks open in rock, the rock's electrical resistance rises because air is not a good conductor of electricity. The cracks also increase the surface area of rock exposed to water; the water thus comes in contact with more radioactive material and absorbs more radon—a radioactive gas that the Soviet scientists had noticed in increased quantities in Garm-area wells. In addition, because the cracking of the rock increases its volume, dilatancy can account for the crustal uplift and tilting that preceded some quakes. The Japanese, for instance, noticed a 2-inch rise in the ground as long as five years before the major quake that rocked Niigata in 1964. Scientists are less certain about how dilatancy accounts for variations in the local magnetic field but think that the effect is related to changes in the rock's electrical resistance.

With their new knowledge, U.S. and Russian scientists cautiously began making private predictions of impending earthquakes. In 1973, after he had studied data from seven portable seismographs at the Blue Mountain Lake encampment, Columbia's Aggarwal excitedly telephoned Lynn Sykes back at the laboratory. All signs, Aggarwal said, pointed to an imminent earthquake of magnitude 2.5 to 3. As Aggarwal was sitting down to dinner two days later, the earth rumbled under his feet. "I could feel the waves passing by," he recalls, "and I was jubilant." In November 1973, after observing changes in P wave velocity, Cal-Tech's Whitcomb predicted that there would be a shock near Riverside, California, within three months. Sure enough, a tremor did hit before his deadline—on January 30th. Whitcomb's successful prediction was particularly important. All previous forecasts had involved quakes along thrust faults, where rock on one side of a fault is pushing against rock on the other. The Riverside quake took place on a strike-slip fault, along which the adjoining sides are sliding past each other. Because most upheavals along the San Andreas fault involve strike-slip quakes, Whitcomb's forecast raised hopes that seismologists could use their new techniques to predict the major earthquakes that are bound to occur along the San Andreas.

The second U.S. quake to be predicted by Caltech geophysicists unfolded in early 1974 at the place and time predicted, but with the wrong magnitude. In a third try not long afterward, Menlo Park scientists monitoring the survey's network of instruments south of Hollister, California, informally predicted a magnitude 5.2 shock that correctly predicted the time of occurrence, but was slightly off in location.

Yet, this was the major American achievement. Seismologist Malcolm Johnston of the U.S. Geological Survey's Earthquake Research Center had casually announced to an informal gathering of U.S.G.S. employees that his figures from data analyzed along seven monitoring stations indicated that perhaps as early as the following day, Hollister could expect a moderate earthquake of up to magnitude 5. The 75 or so geologists and guests could hardly believe their ears. They had assembled for an evening of socializing and routine gossip about faults, core samples, and volcanoes. Instead, they were hearing scientific history in the making. Johnston explained that the strength of the local magnetic field had suddenly risen between two of the stations, then gradually subsided over a period of one week. Furthermore, the surface of the earth in the same area had undergone slight but noticeable changes in tilt. "These changes are just the sort one might expect to see before a quake," he observed.

The next afternoon on November 28, 1974, while residents of Hollister were sitting down to their Thanksgiving Day dinner, the earth began to sway and rumble beneath them. The brief 2 to 3 second quake measured 5.2 magnitude and did little damage. But its impact still reverberates through the world of seismology. The accurate forecast of the Hollister earthquake was an astounding demonstration that scientists are on the verge of being able to predict the time, place, and even the size of earthquakes.

Chinese Prediction of Earthquakes

Perhaps the greatest and most murderous natural disaster in the history of man occurred in Shensi Province in 1556, when an earthquake snuffed out 820,000 lives. In 1920, China's Kansu Province experienced an earthquake that killed some 200,000 people. Since then, the Chinese have compiled a 3,000-year catalogue of their earthquakes, a unique document that some scientists believe can reveal whether quakes occur in identifiable patterns.

Following a particularly bad quake during 1966 in Hsing-T'A', about 200 miles southwest of Peking in Hopei Province, Chinese seismologists launched a major effort to predict the disasters. Chou En-lai, who at that time was Premier, set a priority on seismology and ordered Liu Ying-Yung, director of China's State Seismological Bureau, to develop a huge seismological network. From the start, the approach emphasized grass-roots participation. The feeling was that peasants had accumulated knowledge over the past 3,000 years about those events which precede earthquakes and that information ought to be as much a part of an earthquake prediction system as modern scientific instruments.

Invited to China in October, 1974, a group of U.S. experts led by M.I.T.'s geologist Frank Press was astonished to discover a trained corps of 10,000 earthquake professionals,* aided by 100,000 amateur seismologists. Dr. C. Barry Raleigh of the U.S. Geological Survey and Dr. Lynn Sykes of Lamont-Doherty heard of three successful predictions based on animal behavior; rats leaving buildings, snakes in large numbers crawling from their holes, fowl refusing to go to roost.

Chinese scientists were operating 17 major observation centers, which in turn receive data from 300 seismic stations and 5,000 observation points (some of which are simply wells where the radon content of water is measured). In addition, thousands of dedicated amateurs, mainly high school students, regularly collect earthquake data. By enlisting these amateur observers—some of whom include farmers, workers, teachers, telephone operators, meteorologists and radio broadcasters—the Communists have given the population a role and a stake in placing the common citizen on the same side as the scientist.

---

*Especially in the quake-ravaged provinces of north China.

The Chinese have good reason to be vigilant. Many homes of the people are vulnerable adobe type, tile-roofed homes that collapse easily during tremors. And the country shudders through a great number of earthquakes, apparently because of the northward push of the Indian plate against the Eurasian plate. Says Press, "It is probably the one country that could suffer a million dead in a single earthquake."

Chinese scientists read every scientific paper published by foreign earthquake researchers. They also pay close attention to exotic prequake signals—including oddities of animal behavior—so far largely overlooked by other nations. Before a quake in the summer of 1969, the Chinese observed that in the Tientsin zoo, the swans abruptly left the water, a Manchurian tiger stopped pacing in his cage, a Tibetan Yak collapsed, and a panda held its head in its paws and moaned.

As early as 1970, Chinese seismologists were able to thwart a major earthquake when they identified a region in southern Manchuria as one of seismic threat. Swarming over the area, they closed in on a danger zone surrounding the town of Haich'eng.

From the very start of the program, Liaoning Province looked suspicious. Following the earthquake at Hsingtai, seismologists noted that the epicenter of subsequent smaller shocks seemed to be migrating northeast towards Liaoning, heavily populated and industrialized. In 1970, a decision was taken to keep a close watch on the province. This involved all the techniques in the seismologist's panoply, starting with the study of past earthquakes and local geology.

Geodetic surveying across a major fault between September 1973 and June 1974, showed that the earth's surface there was rising twenty times faster than in a normal year and tilting towards the northwest. During the same period, a change was recorded in the earth's magnetic field and tidal stations on the shore of Liaotung Bay showed a rise in sea level. Finally, the number of small earthquakes in 1974 was five times higher than normal.

By 1974 their instruments showed ever increasing anomalies. Reports of ominous precursors poured in from amateurs—communal wells muddying and bubbling, livestock and dogs behaving strangely, radon counts up. A 4.8 foreshock rumbled, and one area sounded a false alarm. For two nights families obediently slept outside in the Manchurian winter. In February, 1975, tigers in nearby zoos became listless and lethargic, thousands of fish jumped from the nearby rivers to their banks, and the waters of wells began turning red. Chickens panicked, pigs refused to enter pigsties, and horses and sheep ran about frenziedly. Since the farmer was considered to be a valuable source of changes in animal behavior or in the levels of ground water, Chinese seismologists were certain the long feared earthquake was imminent.

But this kind of folk wisdom wasn't the only evidence seismologists were using for their prediction. It was supplemented by some of the most advanced technology the Chinese had, leading Western experts to the conclusion that the Communists had a broad and most agressive program, even though some of their instrumentation lacked the sophistication, precision, and reliability of the free world. Their highly sophisticated technology to monitor a wide variety of physical characteristics that might precede the onset of earthquakes includes observation of minute movements across geological fault lines which are sensed by lasers, slight changes in the tilt and electrical resistance of the earth's crust, decreases in the amount of the radioactive gas radon in well water, and variations in the speeds of seismic waves. Seventeen fully equipped seismographic centers and the 250 auxillary stations have been installed, and earthquake prediction data are being gathered at 5,000 separate locations.

The plan included contingencies to get the Chinese in the area into the open air when the signals suggested an earthquake was imminent since the major cause of the high death rates has been the collapse of homes and other buildings on their occupants.

Although seismologists detected preliminary indications of the disaster as far back as June the preceding year, the warning signs began to multiply three days before the earthquake on February 4. Peasants noticed that water levels in the wells rose suddenly, farm animals refused to enter their folds, and school children skating on frozen lakes observed that frogs were jumping through holes in the ice. Most important, however, scientists noted an abrupt fall in terrestrial electricity and observed a tilt of the earth toward the southwest. Nearby, a hotspring resort's natural flow of water was abruptly cut off. The most peculiar incident took place in the Shaozihe commune in YouYan county when gas-bearing water spouted forth from ice like geysers. Two days later, cadres at the small Yingkou City seismological station detected a series of minor tremors and reported to Peking that a major earthquake seemed imminent. This was the last straw, since the series of small earthquakes that had begun on February 1, had occurred in a region that had been almost non-seismic previously. The seismologists studied the location of the shocks and the direction taken by their so-called P waves (seismic waves that cause rocks in their path to compress and then expand in the same direction as the waves are travelling). The scientists concluded that these were the forerunners of a much larger earthquake to hit the region. Dutifully, the scientists passed their findings on to the local government. An hour and a half later, a meeting in Haiching decided that it was time to move from earthquake maneuvers to reality. At 2 P.M. on February 4, the military commander of Yingkou County's Kuanteng Commune went on the air with an urgent warning. "There probably will be a strong earthquake tonight," he said, "we require all to leave their own homes and animals to leave the fold, also, to move the weak and old. There will be four movies shown outdoors at the city square tonight." Without delay people evacuated their homes and began building temporary huts in the fields. Patients were moved from hospitals, medical teams organized and other units were formed to handle transportation and machine pools. Five and a half hours later, at 7:36 P.M., the quake began.

The tremor registered 7.3 on the Richter scale, indicating that it was far more intense than the major earthquake that devastated the Nicaraguan capital of Managua in 1972. Loss of life, the Chinese reported, was greatly reduced because most people had left their homes. Vehicles had been removed from garages and farm animals from barns. Within the most destructive area, more than 90 percent of the houses collapsed to some extent, but many agricultural brigades did not suffer even a single casualty. Supposedly, in the Dingjiagov brigade of Haicheng, consisting of more than 3,000 people, only one child was injured. On one street in Yingkou, 3,470 persons came through with no casualties— although 82 of their 801 homes collapsed completely. The official Communist report stated: "However, in certain communes and brigades, such as the Shinpengyou brigade, two commune members, influenced by old ideas, did not believe the prediction of a strong earthquake. They brought their children back to sleep in the evening of February 4. As a consequence, among more than 3,400 people in this brigade, three died in the earthquake."

This led the Chinese to conclude that if earthquake losses are to be reduced, one must not only estimate the danger accurately but at the same time educate those who are at risk, making certain that the seismologists' findings do not remain arcane secrets. Their concern about the human side was officially expressed as: "Let seismological work be really considered as the task of the masses of the people as well as of the governmental seismological brigades."

Scientists from across the world were awed by the reported accuracy of the prediction. "Nowhere else in the world had this size earthquake been predicted with this kind of precision," marveled Press. "We now know how they did it."

The system is not always so successful. Communist authorities apparently failed to predict other strong quakes and Chinese seismologists admit to their American colleagues that they have issued some false alarms. But Chinese officials are currently taking precautions in the light of a new prediction—that a damaging earthquake may strike the densely populated area between Peking and Tientsin within the coming years.

"The Chinese success," stated Dr. Robert M. Hamilton, Chief of the U.S. Geological Survey Office of Earthquake Studies, "signals that the age of earthquake prediction may be upon us. As far as those intriguing animal precursors, we were skeptical before our Chinese experience. Now, we've got to reconsider the evidence." On his return from the China tour, U.S.G.S.'s Barry Raleigh learned that horses had behaved skittishly in the Hollister area before the Thanksgiving Day quake. "We were very skeptical when we arrived in China regarding animal behavior," he says, "but there may be something in it."

A similar attitude was expressed by Tagnar Stefansson of the Icelandic Meteorological Office who told how an earthquake swarm had struck the north of his country near the end of last year. Within a month, it generated no fewer than 10,000 earthquakes that could be felt without instruments, 100 of them greater than 4. On December 25, 1975, he was able to tell local sheep-raisers that there was no need to fear any more severe shocks. He emphasized that the population must be involved: "If you explain what you know and what is happening, people won't hold it against you if you make mistakes."

But in China, the ancient superstition which says, "When earthquakes strike, mighty dynasties fall" may not be entirely false. And, that superstition helps explain, at least in part, modern China's extraordinary interest in the science of earthquake prediction. Yet, interest is not enough to guarantee success in any quake prediction effort. For example, although vast numbers of skilled seismologists and volunteer quake-watchers were observing everything from tiny earth tremors and subtle magnetic warnings to the behavior of panic-stricken chickens, the teams failed to predict the devastating 1976 Tangshan earthquake which killed 655,000 people in Hopeh Province just east of Peking. An additional 779,000 were injured and an additional 500,000 left homeless.

Today, the Chinese are forecasting a dozen earthquakes with a magnitude greater than 5 during the next three years. However, this is only a "small percentage" of all that occur because few observations are available from remote areas in western China.

Though the U.S. does not have the national commitment of the Chinese, there is no look of urgency among American scientists. California has not had a great earthquake since the San Francisco disaster in 1906, and seismologists are warily eyeing at least two stretches of the San Andreas fault that seem to be "locked." One segment, near Los Angeles, has apparently not budged, while other parts of the Pacific and North American Plates have slid some 30 feet past each other. Near San Francisco, there is another locked section. Sooner or later such segments will have to catch up with the inexorable movement of the opposing plates. If they do so in one sudden jolt, the resulting earthquakes, probably in the 7- to 8-point Richter range and packing the energy of 50 multimegaton hydrogen bombs, will cause widespread destruction in the surrounding areas.

If one of those quakes occurs in the San Francisco area, the results will be far more calamitous than in 1906. A comparable earthquake near Los Angeles could kill as many as 20,000 and injure nearly 600,000. However, it should be noted that in the United States only 1,600 lives have been lost to earthquakes during the entire history of the country and the typical American wooden dwelling can be expected to ride out most shocks.

What does the Haicheng experience mean for us? To earthquake scientists, it means:

- That science is learning more and more about the kinds of events that can signal coming earthquakes, events which in some cases may begin years or months before major shocks and in others may precede the quakes by only hours.

- That there are highly specific "percursor events" such as foreshocks, ground tilts, water level changes, radon readings, shifts of electric current and magnetic field strength whose more detailed study will inevitably sharpen the accuracy of future quake prediction if they are studied more intensively.

- That a population thoroughly prepared for earthquake warnings (and in the case of the Chinese, subject of course to intense social discipline) can protect itself against injury and death on a massive scale with timely, credible warning.

It is apparent that the Chinese are continuously strengthening their quake prediction effort. And, the closeness of Peking, seat of today's ruling political dynasty, to the tumultuous earthquake ground of Hopeh Province may well account for some of that effort. Dynasties, after all, do fall in public tumult.

History of Earthquake Prediction in the United States

As early as 1960, a large percentage of the seismological research in the United States was part of the Nuclear Test Detection Program of the Advanced Research Projects Agency of the Department of Defense. In many ways, this program converted seismology into a truly unique observational science, using the time arrays of seismic detectors, digital processing of data, and the application of information theory in signal processing. Actually, in its initial stages, the Test Detection Program concentrated primarily upon radical improvements of basic research in seismology and upon the modernization of seismic instruments on a worldwide scale. In 1960, the Worldwide Network of Standard Seismographs, consisting of 130 stations recording both short and long-period information was installed. The brilliant worldwide nature of the network, coupled with the availability of microfilm records and the sensitivity of the instruments used, literally revolutionized the experimental side of seismological research.

After the tragic 1964 Alaskan earthquake, an ad hoc panel of eminent scientists appointed by President Johnson drew up a 10-year plan for a major U.S. earthquake prediction program. Both the U.S. Geological Survey and the U.S. Coast and Geodetic Survey began small-scale efforts in research during the next year. Interest immediately rose among university scientists who were supported by the National Science Foundation. However, no major federal effort was launched in terms of earthquake prediction until 1973 when funds were added to the budgets of the U.S. Geological Survey and the seismological research efforts of the National Oceanic and Atmospheric Administration of the Department of Commerce.

By 1973, American seismological researchers began to turn their full attention to earthquake prediction because of such funding as well as the promising prediction results of the observations by scientists in Japan, China, and the U.S.S.R. The year before, a U.S.-U.S.S.R. Working Group in Earthquake Prediction was established under the aegis of the 1972 agreement between the two nations cooperating in the field of environmental protection. Establishing a small, yet vigorous program of joint field, laboratory, analytical, and theoretical studies in earthquake prediction, the work was organized into four main areas: A) field investigations of earthquake prediction; B) laboratory and theoretical investigations of earthquake sources; C) mathematical and computational prediction of places where large earthquakes occur and evaluations of seismic risks; and D) engineering seismological investigations.

In the meantime, earthquake prediction information was being exchanged with Japan under the guidance of the National Science Foundation.

In late 1973, the National Science Foundation became a major source of support for engineering seismology and for research into public policy issues related to earthquake prediction. The U.S. Nuclear Regulatory Commission began supporting seismological research into seismic hazards to nuclear power plants as well as the seismological criteria for determining nuclear power plants. Later that year, the National Aeronautics and Space Administration initiated a long-range program geared to adapting the latest space program technologies for possible future uses in earthquake predictions and hazard reduction.

As a practical start toward earthquake prediction, U.S.G.S. is constructing a prototype network of 200 automated sensing stations equipped with magnetometers, tiltmeters, and seismographs in California's Bear Valley. Along the San Andreas fault in California, 50 tiltmeters have been installed in deep and shallow holes while laser-ranging instruments sensitive enough to detect a fraction of an inch of crustal deformation over ten miles have been set up. These tiltmeters have shown the most promise. Since November, 1974, three earthquakes of magnitude 4 or greater on the San Andreas fault were all preceded by a tilt anomaly. About a month before an earthquake, the instruments will start to deflect and keep on deflecting until it occurs.

U.S.G.S. scientists are also beginning to take measurements of radon in wells and electrical resistance in rock. Some of the data is already being fed into the U.S.G.S.'s

A laser ranging device for precisely measuring distances between two points for strain calculation.

central station at Menlo Park, California. But analysis is still being delayed by lack of adequate computer facilities.

Other seismic monitoring grids in the U.S. include a 130-station network in the Los Angeles area, operated jointly by the U.S.G.S. and Caltech; smaller networks in the New York region under the Lamont-Doherty scientists; and those in the Charleston, S.C. area, operated by the University of South Carolina. Stations are also being constructed in Yellowstone National Park, Utah, Missouri, Seattle, Alaska, and Hawaii. When completed and computerized, these experimental networks* could provide two warnings of impending quakes. If scientists detect changes in P wave velocities, magnetic field and other dilatancy effects that persist over a wide area, a large quake can be expected—but not for many months. If the dilatancy effects occur in a small area, the quake will be minor but will occur soon. The return to normal of the dilatancy effects provides the second warning. It indicates that the quake will occur in about one-tenth the

---

*Not as yet operational.

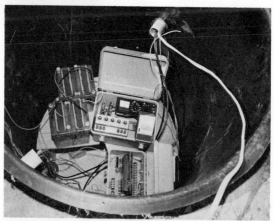

Tiltmeters measuring tilt of the earth.

time during which the changes were measured. If dilatance changes have been recorded for 70 days and then suddenly return to normal, the quake should occur in about a week.

The networks are far from complete, progress in general has been slow and seismologists blame inadequate government funding. The U.S.G.S.'s annual quake budget has remained at about $11 million for the past few years, although less than half is for research in the art of prediction. Other budgetary segments go into researching how best to reduce human and property loss. Another main interest is in earthquake control, that is, devising ways to induce rocks under strain to slide past each other harmlessly instead of locking until a quake builds.

Once in operation, an earthquake warning system will bring with it a new set of problems. How will people react to earthquake forecasts? Could disruption caused by a prediction be worse than the quake itself? What of a false alarm? If a major quake is forecast for San Francisco, for example, should the government shut down business and evacuate the populace? Where would evacuees be housed? If the quake did occur, who will be responsible for the financial loss caused by the evacuation? Answers come more easily in totalitarian China. There, says Press, "If an actual quake does not take place, it is felt that the people will understand that the state is acting on their behalf and accept a momentary disruption in their normal lives." Dr. Ralph H. Turner of U.C.L.A. who headed a National Academy of Science study, does not deny such problems could occur. "We're not talking about total evacuation of cities. If people are protected from fire and collapsing structures, if water levels in dams can be lowered, very few lives need to be lost, even in a strong quake.

At Caltech's prestigious Seismological Laboratory in Pasadena, geophysicist Don Anderson indicated that promising insights into understanding the anatomy of the living earth are coming from the outer universe. He said, "In an arrangement with N.A.S.A., we use two radio-telescope receivers—one at Goldstone in the Mojave Desert and one here in Pasadena—to record radio emissions from Quasars as far as a billion light years away. By precisely comparing the arrival times of an emission, we can detect earth movements between the two stations with enough accuracy to discover precursors of large quakes.

One such warning may lie uncomfortably close at hand. Receiving past elevation surveys, U.S.G.S. geologist Robert O. Castle discovered that a vast area of southern California stretching from the Pacific Ocean to the Mojave Desert has uplifted ten inches in the past 15 years. Known as the "bubble," the area centers on a stretch of the San Andreas fault that has been quiet since a titanic 1857 earthquake rent the surface for 200 miles.

Does the bubble portend another giant tremor? Noting that uplift can occur without a quake, the U.S.G.S. has assigned a task force to keep watch with additional instruments.

Convinced that "earthquake prediction is a fact at the present time," and worried about the effect of such forecasts, particularly in U.S. cities, the National Academy of Sciences released a massive study called "Earthquake Prediction and Public Policy." Prepared by a panel of experts headed by U.C.L.A. sociologist Ralph Turner, the study takes a strong issue with the politicians and the few scientists who believe that earthquake predictions and warnings would cause panic and economic paralysis, thus resulting in more harm than the tremors themselves. Forecasting would clearly save lives, the panel states and that is the "highest priority." Because most casualties during a quake are caused by collapsing buildings, the report recommends stronger building codes in areas where earthquakes occur frequently, the allocation of funds for strengthening existing structures in areas where earthquakes have been forecast and even requiring some of the population to live in mobile homes and tents when a quake is imminent. Fearful that forecasting could become a political football and that some officials might try to suppress news of an impending quake, the panel recommends that warnings, which would cause disruption of daily routine when an earthquake threatens, should be issued by elected officials—but only after a public prediction has been made by a panel of scientists set up by a federal agency.

Other scientists are already looking ahead toward an even more remarkable goal than forecasting earthquake control. What may become the basic technique for taming quakes was discovered accidentally in 1966 by earth scientists in the Denver area. They noted that the forced pumping of lethal wastes from the manufacture of nerve gases into deep wells at the Army's Rocky Mountain arsenal coincided with the occurrence of small quakes in the area. After the forced pumping was halted the number of quakes declined sharply.

Fascinated by the implications of what were apparently man-made quakes, U.S.G.S. scientists in 1969 set up their instruments at the Rangley oil field in northwestern Colorado. There, Chevron was recovering oil from less productive wells by injecting water into them under great pressure. The recovery technique was setting off small quakes, the strongest near the wells subjected to the greatest water pressure. If water was pumped out of the earth, the survey scientists wondered, would the quakes stop? In November, 1972, they forced water into four of the Chevron wells. A series of minor quakes soon began and did not stop until March of 1973 when the scientists pumped water out of the wells, reducing fluid pressure in the rock below. Almost immediately earthquake activity ended. In a limited way they had controlled an earthquake.

The results of the Rangley experiments led U.S.G.S. geophysicists Raleigh and James Dietrich to propose an ingenious scheme. They suggested drilling a row of three deep holes about 500 yards apart along a potentially dangerous fault. By pumping water out of the outer holes, they figured they could effectively strengthen the surrounding rock and lock the fault at each of those places. Then they would inject water into the middle hole, increasing fluid pressure in the nearby rocks and weakening them to the point of failure. A minor quake—contained between the locked areas—should result, relieving the dangerous stresses in the immediate vicinity. By repeating the procedure the scientists could eventually relieve strains over a wide area. Other scientists feel that such experiments should be undertaken with caution, lest they trigger a large quake. Raleigh is more hopeful. In theory, he says, relatively continuous movement over the entire length of the San Andreas fault could be controlled and major earthquakes prevented—with a system of some 500 three-mile deep holes evenly spaced along the fault. Estimated cost of the gigantic project: $1 to $2 billion.

However, in a time of austerity, the possibility of such lavish financing is remote. As M.I.T.'s Press puts it: "How does one sell preventive medicine for a future afflicition to government agencies beleaguered with current illness?" Ironically, the one event that would release money for the study of earthquake prediction and control is the very disaster that scientists are trying to avert: a major quake striking a highly populated area without any warning. Tens of thousands of people living in the flood plain of the Van Norman Dam had a close call a few years ago in the San Fernando Valley quake. Had the tremor lasted a few more seconds, the dam might have given way. When the San Andreas fault convulses again—as surely it must—or when another less notorious fault elsewhere in the U.S. suddenly gives way, thousands of other Americans may not be so lucky.

The Public and Earthquake Prediction

At the present level of technology, earthquakes cannot be prevented. Nor for some years to come will it be possible to predict them in the detail required to safeguard the people and economy of a nation. Some scientists are optimistic that if all goes well, however, we may have success in about ten years in being able to actually predict when an earthquake will strike. Even then, say the optimists, it means favorable governmental funding and, at that, we'll never be able to come up with a single device that signals GREEN when we are safe and flashes RED when danger threatens. But prediction is certainly possible. And it will succeed in saving lives and property.

Earthquake prediction was a constant preoccupation for the early soothsayer, astrologer, or prophet, and indeed there are many instances recorded in history of destructive earthquakes having been forecasted. Once looked upon with suspicion, earthquake prediction has in the last few years become a scientifically respectable topic. And, even when accurate, such predictions are not likely to be effective. In the past, people seemed strangely reluctant to believe that an earthquake will occur whether it is a credited astrologer or a seismologist who tells them so.

History is full of such examples, demonstrating that man reacts to an inevitable hazard in a special way distinct from a preventable hazard. The earthquake of A.D. 1042 in Tabriz, Iran, was predicted by the chief astrologer who tried in vain to persuade the people to leave. Earthquakes had happened in Tabriz sufficiently frequently to be likely to occur again, yet the main reaction to the prediction was one of apathy. The earthquake happened and more than 40,000 people perished. Subsequent predictions, allegedly accurate, were invariably ignored.

The earthquake of 1549 in eastern Iran was also predicted by the local Cadi (judge) who tried unsuccessfully to convince his people to stay out in the open that particular night. They refused to listen and the Cadi stayed out alone, but finding the night very cold returned to his house where he soon perished with 3,000 people in the district. Apparently, the Cadi himself was not too sure about his prediction.

Scientists now feel that with earthquakes, it is not only the prediction and warning problems that are important, but also the social and economic implications of forecasting such disasters. False alarms and inaccurate timing might create more problems than already exist. Although scientists would welcome earthquake prediction, it is not certain whether it would solve more problems for the general public than the social, economic, and even political ones that it will create.

There is no denying that there is at present a lack of knowledge regarding earthquake risk in many parts of the world, and it is through the study of the historical record that such facts may become known. In spite of the recent rapprochement between archaeologists, historians and earth scientists, a proper alliance for the study of subjects of mutual interest such as early earthquakes, volcanic eruptions, weather changes, droughts, and floods, has not been formed.

Work on these subjects is being pursued singly and with little cooperation or guidance from other fields of knowledge, a process which is not only painfully slow and inefficient, but one which is fraught with danger of misuse of other disciplines.

The need for a coordinated research program on historical earthquakes and other natural hazards is obvious. Such research, the scope of which is international and global, will give further dimension to our knowledge of what nature has in store for us.

Thus, the rudimentary science of earthquake prediction will probably see substantial advances in the next two decades. Prediction may improve with respect to probable time of occurrence, location, and perhaps magnitude of some future earthquakes, but it will take much longer before most earthquakes can be anticipated accurately. Indeed, some important earthquakes may never be predicted accurately.

Earthquake Prediction: A Definition

What actually constitutes an earthquake prediction?

A worthwhile earthquake prediction must specify the expected magnitude range, the geographical area within which it will occur, and the time interval within which it will happen with sufficient precision so that meaningful social action can be taken. Only by careful recording and analysis of failures as well as successes can the eventual success of the total effort be evaluated and future directions determined. Moreover, scientists should also assign a confidence level to each prediction. It is clear that particularly in the early stages of the effort some predictions will merit considerably greater assurance than others, but even low-confidence predictions should be considered and evaluated. A prediction of locality without specification of time, while valuable in itself, and constituting the principal basis of present-day seismic zoning maps, is not an acceptable prediction in the sense that the word is used by scientists.

It is clear that the time uncertainty for some predictions will necessarily be much greater than for others. Very broad time predictions, for example, "within 25 years," can have significant value in encouraging permanent social responses such as the development of realistic building codes, land-use planning, and long-term disaster preparation. Nevertheless, scientists recognize that the word "prediction" is more commonly interpreted, particularly by the public, to imply a much smaller time uncertainty. The expression "short term prediction" means an earthquake prediction which has a sufficiently precise time estimate, close enough to the time at which the prediction is made, so that significant social responses are possible. This means the preparation of emergency forces and evacuation of questionable structures.

Even in the absence of evidence adequate to permit a low-confidence prediction, unexplained geophysical anomalies in a given area may still be of sufficient concern to cause it to be designated as an "area of intensive study." This designation has been used in Japan to avoid undue public alarm in situations where no realistic prediction is possible in spite of recognized anomalies that are possible precursors to arthquakes and that clearly warrant accelerated investigation. But obviously any capability for reliable prediction, no matter how long the time span, is more useful than none at all.

Today, two methods of study are being used by scientists in their efforts to predict earthquakes—statistical and geophysical methods. The statistical method uses the cataloged history of earthquakes in a region as a key to estimating when and where such future events may occur. The geophysical method involves the observation and interpretation of certain changes in the physical environment in earthquake prone regions as indications of an impending event.

A third method gaining more respect with scientists is that analysis conducted by the quake detective. For example, geologist Diana Dale is rewriting seismic history. In the past 24 years she has single-handedly erased three legendary earthquakes off the official records and has relocated two others. She says, "It is standard to investigate an area for seismic history when a nuclear power plant, or any other major structure, is projected. Validation of every report of an earthquake in the days before reliable records is part of the check."

Dale works for Bechtel's hydro and community facilities division. Her latest challenge has been in the Wenatchee-Lake Chelan area of central Washington where she is relocating an 1872 quake, safely away from Puget Sound where it was once placed and where a nuclear plant is planned. She says,

> It is no coincidence that I seem to have cornered the earth-quake detecting market here. The day in March 1974 when I came to work here, a question came up about the

safety of a power project in east Texas and I drew the assignment. The Rusk, Texas, quake occurred about midnight on a stormy January night in 1891 and involved violent shaking of buildings and a few toppled chimneys at only one location. I collected a vast amount of geological and meteorological information, then talked with old-timers and finally went through ancient diaries and yellowed files of district newspapers. Everything pointed to the tornado that moved through the area that night rather than an earthquake. The U.S. government records first picked up the earthquake report from a story in the *London Times* which got it from a Dallas paper. Once in the record, the error was perpetuated. However, a newspaper in a neighboring town ridiculed it with "the persons from Rusk who fancied they felt the shock had probably not adopted New Year's resolutions," apparently referring to their drinking habits.

Dale's sleuthing on this case enabled her to write a safety analysis report which suggested the nuclear project could move ahead. The public, she insists, should be aware of the geological reality of an area to set regional safety standards for all buildings.

Documenting or discrediting earthquakes is satisfying detective work. In Alabama, for instance, she discovered what was supposed to have been an earthquake in Gadsden in 1905 was really caused by 10 cases of dynamite and powder exploding at nearby Tumlin Gap, where a large tunnel was being cut through a mountain.

Once Dale has determined what happened, she changes or alters the official record in *Earthquake History of the United States* and other public documents. Occasionally, she encounters sticky professional attitudes of other geologists who have accepted the original designation. Earthquake scientists are now encouraging her to interview the elderly, who are reservoirs of knowledge no one has ever bothered to tap. Her grassroots techniques find her in climbing clothes tramping over fault lines in remote spots or investigating mountain rock formations. In central Washington, Dale is learning Indian lore and the stories the tribes passed on after the quakes. To many scientists, she is indeed a "ground breaker and a pioneer."

As we have seen, knowledge of fundamental geological processes, the recognition of global phenomenon of sea floor spreading and continental drift, and the development of the theory of plate tectonics have revolutionized geology. During the next decade, geoscientists may well produce a new kind of map categorizing active faults, especially in California, with respect to the general level of seismic activity that can be expected along each of these breaks.

Consequently, it seems certain that scientists will successfully evaluate the probabilities of occurrence and size of future earthquakes in various parts of California far more effectively in the future than we do now, although it will take longer before most individual earthquakes can be predicted. Prediction, of course, requires "fine grained" and reasonably precise seismic knowledge and theory, while probability estimates can rest on a more generalized understanding of geologic phenomena and history.

Progress in prediction will depend partly on the resources applied to research. While emphasizing this point, however, experts use cautious language with respect to predicting large earthquakes and also warn that the public may be expecting results sooner than is feasible. Certainly, the apparent public impression that routine prediction of earthquakes is imminent is not warranted by the present level of scientific understanding.

Over the years, proposals for prediction techniques have proliferated, drawing relationships between earthquakes and such phenomena as variation in the earth's magnetic and gravity fields, changes in water levels in wells, and even the occurrence of lightning.

The most obvious method of studying the potential for

earthquakes is to measure the accumulation of strain along a fault. Earthquakes, as we know, result from the sudden release of built-up stress in the earth's crust. Sudden changes in the amount of strain, measured by various instruments such as strainmeters placed along the fault, may be precursors of earthquakes. Prior to a destructive Japanese quake in 1964, 15 out of 20 instruments recorded a vertical expansion of the ground.

Another form of crustal deformation is ground tilt. In 1943, a Japanese seismologist obtained a record showing anomalous ground tilt for several days preceding a Japanese quake. The record shows a gradual increase in tilt up to the occurrence of the quake.

A similar observation was reported recently by three California scientists. They had found that about 29 days before the first of two earthquakes that struck Danville, California, in 1971, the entire San Francisco Bay area began to tilt slightly in the general direction of the quake epicenter, increasing steadily up to 10 hours before the tremor actually occurred.

Some scientists have suggested that the pattern of minor seismic activity preceding an earthquake may be a forecasting element. Laboratory studies of rocks under pressure show anomalous strain release prior to rupture very similar to the strain release observed prior to small earthquakes.

Similarly, recurrence curves have been plotted for various faults, such as the San Andreas fault, showing the frequency with which earthquakes of a given magnitude occur along the fault.

Several studies have suggested that world seismic activity has varied with time. About 25 years ago, Dr. Hugo Benioff made a summation of the strain released by the largest earthquakes and noticed five periods of high seismic activity between 1904 and 1951, each separated by quieter periods and each of successively shorter duration. Other scientists have plotted against time the cumulative fault movement throughout the world since 1897. They found that earth-quake activity prior to 1908 was much greater than it has been since that time, and that this pattern is worldwide. Since activity is now below that of the average for the past several million years, they conclude, an increase in seismic activity can be expected in the future. More than 30 years ago, Japanese scientists noted that certain great earthquakes were accompanied by marked changes in the configuration of the earth's magnetic field. A little over an hour before the disastrous Alaskan earthquake of 1964, there was a magnetic field disturbance. Such magnetic changes could be the result of the effect of stress on the magnetic susceptibility of rock masses.

Ultimate settlement of the question of whether local magnetic changes do precede earthquakes has had to await development of more sensitive magnetometers. Such an instrument was developed early last year by two scientists from the Environmental Science Services Administration's research laboratories and a colleague from the Joint Institute for Laboratory Astrophysics at Boulder, Colorado. The new magnetometer will be used operationally for the first time in a study of the effects of reservoir loading on the local magnetic field at Grand Coulee Dam in Washington. The device is ten times more accurate than the best instruments currently in continuous use.

Another recurring proposal is the monitoring of subterranean gases. In the late 1960s, a German geologist successfully predicted an aftershock to an earthquake in southern Germany by observing an abnormal concentration of methane gas in a research shaft. He surmised that earth movements of the kind that precede quakes were permitting a greater than usual amount of the gas to rise through a fault. A rare radioactive gas, radon, was used by the Chinese in a similar manner.

In some parts of the world, earthquakes are often accompanied by various forms of lightning. Scientists recently suggested that this correlation may be due to the ability of quartz in the earth's crust to develop electrical charges when subjected to elastic deformation, as in a quake. Observations of electrical precursors to earthquakes, they propose, may be useful in prediction.

All these environmental anomalies are precursors of earthquakes that may be instrumentally detected, but no single one of them will do an adequate job. What scientists are aiming for now is a thorough understanding of the physical processes, the materials involved, and an adequate monitoring system that will determine the physical state of a region at any given time.

Scientists have also noted that survivors of earthquakes have reported that the earth itself made great noises. History repeats their observation. In recent years, it has been described as the sound of rain. A turn-of-the-century British scientist said it resembled the sound of a cart full of stones turned over, or an immense covey of partridge on the wing. More often, however, it has been compared to the noise of distant thunder. Scientists now concur that these reports are not the result of imagination or the sound of buildings falling down. It seems that the surface of the earth acts like a giant loudspeaker. As a result, the air often fills with a deep rumbling so low in pitch it is often barely above the threshold of human hearing. U.S. Geological Survey geophysicist David P. Hill described the first known recording of the noise, a three-second-long rumbling in the Imperial Valley. It was captured after Geological Survey technician John Coakley spent all night keeping a casette tape recorder going during a period of intense earthquake activity. The research also found that this sound can precede any perceptible shaking by several seconds, which indicates you can literally hear earthquakes coming. The explanation for the early arrival of the sound is that the noise is carried through the earth by compression waves, which travel faster than shear waves, the usual source of earthshaking. Hill called the recording more of a curiosity than a valuable scientific discovery. However, he speculated that some types of noises may eventually be used to help predict earthquakes. Some earthquake specialists have theorized that in the days or weeks preceding earthquakes, large sections of rock deep underground may become filled with fissures a few feet long. It is possible, Hill said, that the formation of the fissures is accompanied by a snapping noise audible at the surface. "You wouldn't really notice it," he said, "but if we were to start looking for them, who knows?"

Observational Capabilities for Earthquake Prediction

The success of U.S. earthquake prediction methods depends upon various kinds of field observation factors such as instrumentation, seismic stations, crustal strain, and elevation measurements.

For example, strainmeters, geochemical monitoring instruments, and three different wavelength electro-optical ranging devices are in use, although they still require development. Even newer and more accurate instruments have been proposed, especially if they can be installed at adequate depths for the elimination of environmental noise effects. At present, though, a wide variety of sensors have been deployed as seismologists research the possibility of adding more satellites and extra-terrestrial positioning systems to the Lageos (an acronym for Laser Geodynamic Satellite) satellite launched by the National Aeronautics and Space Administration (NASA) in 1976. Lageos employs a laser ranging system which measures the roundtrip travel time of a very short, high-energy light pulse to a target, the satellite, equipped with retroflectors which return the light pulse to its source along the same path. Laser ranging using a satellite gives geologists, and other scientists, a benchmark by which they can make highly accurate measurements between relative points of interest on the earth's surface.

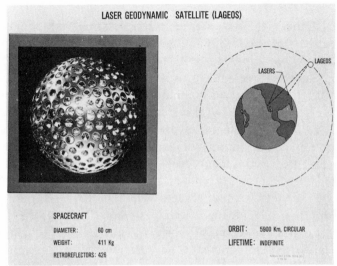

LASER GEODYNAMIC SATELLITE (LAGEOS)

LAGEOS

LASERS

SPACECRAFT

DIAMETER: 60 cm

WEIGHT: 411 Kg

RETROREFLECTORS: 426

ORBIT: 5900 Km, CIRCULAR

LIFETIME: INDEFINITE

Virtually all of the nation's field-monitoring efforts are concentrated in California. Thus far, more than 300 seismic stations have been installed for prediction experiments as well as the location of small daily earthquakes. Hopefully, the measurement of these small earthquakes will be useful in prediction. Approximately 150 other instruments have been installed along California's active faults for the continuous monitoring of strain, tilt and fault creep. But because these instruments are too sparsely distributed, no clear precursory signal has been detected by more than one or two instruments for a given earthquake. At present, the networks can be expected to record an earthquake of magnitude 5-plus in a densely instrumented area every three to four years. Similar instruments have been installed in Alaska, Nevada, Utah, Missouri, Washington and New York.

Meanwhile, over 1,200 established lines with an average length of 20 km have been measured by laser-ranging devices to reveal the accuracies of their strains. Some 500 such lines are measured every year, primarily in California and Nevada. After an interval of five years, the laser measurement is repeated. Such leveling data recently revealed the up and down life of the Palmdale Bulge.

Other field measurements are constantly taking place by members of the U.S. Geological Survey. For example, measurements are made intermittently along a 40 km section of the San Andreas fault in order to determine its electrical resistivity. Also, radon emanation from soils and subsurface waters is monitored weekly over 30 sites in California. An array of 7 magnetometers with ¼ gamma sensitivity is functioning in a continuously recording manner in the densely instrumented section near Hollister.

Surveying with magnetometers by registering differences at sites 10 km apart has been conducted semi-annually along two of California's longest lines. This is perhaps the least expensive technique for analyzing longterm changes in local fields. Gravimeter surveys engineered to determine elevation changes greater than a few centimeters are also now possible. A few wells in the Hollister area are now being monitored for ground water level variations due to the Chinese success with the method.

Most of the conceptual underpinnings of the physical models now used to explain earthquake precursors have been derived from laboratory experiments. A few years ago, the dilatancy and precursory fault creep was observed in lab studies. The search for other precursors such as seismic velocity, changes in electrical resistivity, and microseismicity was begun by scientists in the U.S. and Japan less than 10 years ago under controlled conditions available to laboratory experimentalists. The precursory phenomena noticed in the field have guided the researchers to a clearer understanding of the physical bases of earthquake phenomena.

Today, most current research focuses on the details of the failure process preceding brittle fracture. Dilatant cracking and fault creep generally precede sudden failure and accelerate unstably near the time fracture occurs. New "laboratory earthquakes" are underway to analyze these processes at greater than room temperature. Also, studies of faulting as a dislocation along a sliding surface between two large

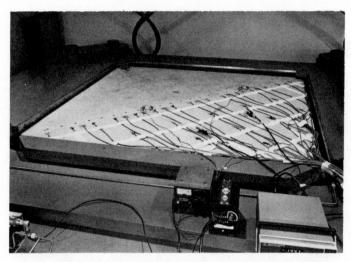

An earthquake control experiment is taking place. A 4' x 2' rock sample with a fault cut diagonally across the sample. When the rock is stressed in the frame shown, small earthquakes occur on the fault. The strain in the rock prior and during the earthquake is measured by numerous small strain gauges wired to a central recorder.

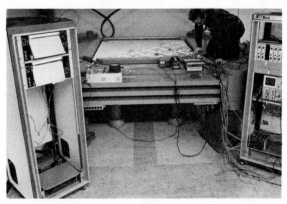

Quentin A. Gorten, the research and development engineer who engineered the rock sample testing device, kneels to check the hydraulic pressure system.

Apparatus for deforming rocks at high temperatures and pressures and locating small earthquakes within the rocks as they deform and ultimately break.

blocks are now under way and should yield direct observation of precursory phenomena and earthquake source parameters.

Chimpanzees Predict Earthquakes

Recently, behavioral scientists at Stanford University's School of Medicine discovered that the 15 chimpanzees in their outdoor primate facility could predict earthquakes. Opened in 1974, the facility is located near the Jasper Ridge Biological Preserve and has been used by researchers and students to observe social behavior and hormonal changes among chimps in a well-planned, natural setting. But, Stanford adminstrators had inadvertently built the facility adjacent to the San Andreas fault. Thus, an ideal model was created for studying the relationship of animal behaviors to earthquakes.

In late October of 1976, Dr. Helena Kraemer, associate professor of biostatistics in the Department of Psychiatry and Behavioral Sciences, reported at a meeting sponsored by the U.S. Geological Survey in Menlo Park that "while our evidence is not yet sufficient to conclude that chimpanzee behavior will predict earthquakes, it suggests a model for researching the question."

Interested in investigating popular reports of unusual animal behavior prior to a temblor, as well as Chinese claims of predicting earthquakes by observing insect, fish, and animal behaviors, Kraemer and other Stanford scientists began observing the animals. In early June of that year, she observed intriguing behavioral changes among the chimpanzees prior to a single swarm of minor earthquakes.

> The animals were more restless than usual. They spent more time on the ground than high in their climbing structures and nesting areas. Their behavior change was so significant it seemed unlikely it was due to change. At the time we recorded animal behavior, we were doing unrelated research. And, a little later, we were unaware that any tremors had occurred.

Acting upon a suggestion by geophysicist Bruce Smith of the U.S. Geological Survey, Dr. Kraemer and Dr. Seymour Levine, director of the Stanford Primate Center, analyzed the course of chimpanzee behavior before and after 25 minor earthquakes which occurred in the Palo Alto vicinity between June 19 and 24, 1975. The two researchers found that behavior changed significantly on the day prior to two of the largest earthquakes during the five day period. One temblor occurred on June 19 and registered 3.1 on the

WHY CAN I PREDICT EARTHQUAKES
AND O.E.S. CANNOT ?

Richter scale. The other earthquake occurred on June 24 and measured 2.0. In both cases, signs of restlessness and change in location by the chimps had occurred the day before. However, such behavioral changes were less pronounced in the in-between period during which the area was experiencing tremors of lesser intensity.

> Animal behaviors can be monitored and reliably measured. We believe we have the first scientific evidence there are behavior changes that precede earthquakes. Obviously, to prove it conclusively, we will have to predict the next earthquake. Multiple monitors will be needed using less expensive animals such as poultry and cattle scattered along the major faults. Trained observers or automated behavior monitors will be required, coupled with computerized systems for routine observation and data analysis.

In addition to this, say seismologists, the behaviors of each animal species will have to be analyzed and intelligent decisions made as to the magnitude of change warranting an

Observing behavior changes in chimpanzees has paid·an unexpected dividend for Dr. Seymour Levine and Dr. Helena C. Kraemer of the Stanford Department of Psychiatry and Behavioral Sciences. The scientists reported in October of 1976 that they had obtained scientific evidence that chimpanzees may be used to predict earthquakes. The research is conducted at the Stanford Outdoor Primate Facility located adjacent to the San Andreas fault.

Chimpanzees are shown on the primate facility grounds. Stanford University scientists have obtained scientific evidence that certain changes in chimpanzee behavior during 1976 preceded earthquakes in the area.

earthquake alert. Amos Nur, a Stanford geophysicist, feels that animal behavior studies will comprise the most important single effort in earthquake prediction during the next few years. Nur was among those who conferred with Chinese scientists after they had predicted the major earthquake in Haicheng during 1975.

The Stanford primate facility is operated and staffed in conjunction with the Laboratory of Stress and Conflict in the Department of Psychiatry and Behavioral Sciences in the School of Medicine. Costing $408,000 for the four quadrants of 1½ acres each containing trees, climbing structures, nesting areas, objects for manipulation, etc., the modern facility was supported by gifts from private foundations and individuals.

How Animals, Reptiles, Fish, and Insects Predict Earthquakes

Chickens refused to roost. Dogs barked uncontrollably. Horses refused to eat. Cattle in barns bellowed and pulled at their chains. Snakes crawled out of the ground. Deer flocked down from the mountains. Rats ran into the streets dazed and allowed people to stomp on them. Caged birds flew amok. Tigers in zoos roared voraciously. Cuckoos cried in the fields and uttered sounds never heard from them before.

Bizarre as they seem, all these forms of behavior happened hours before earthquakes devastated northern Italy, China, and Guatemala. So much has been learned by scientists about animal and insect behavior prior to an earthquake that Dr. Barry Raleigh, a geophysicist for the U.S. Geological Survey said recently,

> The animals are doing great. I only wish they could talk about it and explain what they sense. All over the world today there is much observation of animals around earthquake faults. When earthquakes occurred in Chile in 1822 and 1825, large numbers of seagulls were said to sense the coming shocks and swooped strangely inland.

Indeed, such phenomena is not new. Before a 1935 earthquake in Talcahuco, Mexico, dogs were said to run howling through the streets. In 1906, San Franciscans noted the same phenomena. Before a massive earthquake struck the southern Philippines in 1976, dogs, cats, and cows created a cacophony of yelps, howls, and bellows.

The first documented scientific statement that fish can sense the coming of an earthquake was laid out in a paper published by the Japanese Imperial Academy in 1932 by two scientists. Studying the behavior of catfish, they learned that the catfish began to dart and swim nervously in ponds before the tremors occurred. Today, it is known that fish can sense the coming of an earthquake because the stress on the earth's crust produces a change in the electric fields they perceive. The electric fields are perceived by fish in much the same way that knocking on a fish tank produces a reaction of skittish behavior in an aquarium.

Indeed, Gary Latham, a geophysicist for the University of Texas, is trying to startle goldfish into leaping out of their tanks so he can devise a system to warn people of uncoming earthquakes. He got the idea while in Guatemala studying the after-effects of a quake which killed over 17,000 people in 1975. He met a man who lived about 20 miles from the center of the devastating tremor. The man had apparently gotten up a few minutes past midnight to eat a snack and was astonished to see his two goldfish leap straight out of their bowl and land on the floor. Puzzled, the man replaced the fish in their bowl and went back to sleep. Three hours later, Guatemala was shaken by the strong earthquake.

Latham feels sure the goldfish somehow sensed the coming of that tremor and the thought has stirred his imagination. People in earthquake-prone areas might save their lives and possessions by keeping goldfish and evacuating their homes when the fish go into a frenzy. Latham reasons:

> Certainly series of tiny cracks occur in the rocks preceding a quake. This cracking must be accompanied by slight

ground vibrations and sounds that humans may not be able to hear. Changes in the earth's electric and magnetic fields probably take place. Animals, fish, reptiles, insects may sense one or all of these things. We know animals tune into geophysical stimuli that are beyond human senses. Birds, for example, navigate by using the earth's magnetic field.

Of course, the association between odd animal behavior and earthquakes is not new. Chinese seismologists have long used observations of animal behavior to supplement their sophisticated instruments in trying to predict quakes and Japanese scientists are currently studying various kinds of fish for the same purpose. Indeed, cockroaches may even have such productive value. A Western diplomat stationed in the Tangshan region of China could not sleep one night and went to his kitchen for a glass of milk when he noticed a sea of cockroaches coming toward him. The nocturnal insects had apparently climbed several floors of piping a few hours before. The thousands of roaches appeared to be fleeing from something. At about this moment in another part of the region, another observer noticed cats with their fur standing on end for no apparent reason. A few minutes later, a 7.5 Richter scale quake hit.

Also, the notion that dogs begin howling before an earthquake may not be an old wives' tale. It seems that dogs indeed begin complaining at the first sign of an earthquake. There might be some precursor of a major quake that people don't feel, but that dogs and other animals and insects sense because they have a slightly lower threshold.

In October of 1976, the government awarded a $23,000 contract to U.C.L.A. to monitor behavior of rats and mice near the San Andreas fault in San Bernardino county. Other animal study contracts may soon be awarded.

Jack Evernden, contracts and grant manager of the U.S. Geological Survey's Office of Earthquake Studies in Menlo Park commented on animal behavior prior to an earthquake:

The evidence is so massive that animals sense something, I guess I'd have to say I was convinced. I have gathered over 200 reports from all over the Bay area of unusual animal behavior before the January 8 Oakland-Berkeley quake which measured 4.6 on the Richter scale. The number and diversity of the accounts astonishes me. All this new information could help us decide to set up animal warning centers in California.

Recently, it was concluded that animals were probably detecting a change in the atmosphere's electrostatic field, although the possibility the animals smelled gas being expelled from the ground was not dismissed. Reluctantly, scientists have rejected the possibility that animals may have heard the fracturing of underground rocks before the final tearing shock.

Added Evernden, "Essentially there is no possibility an animal can hear an earthquake that a person can't hear. Also, I don't believe it's anything psychic. But there is something out there that's measurable. I only wish I knew what to measure!"

Recently, when seismologists gathered at the National Earthquake Research Center in Menlo Park, excitement centered around reports of unusual animal behavior prior to the August 1, 1976 earthquake in Oroville, California. There, rats infested homes, parrots and parakeets fell off their perches or flew about wildly, squirrels acted crazily, fish swam in unusual patterns, a turtle laid an egg for the first time, horses, goats, and cattle acted peculiarly in their corrals or refused to enter their barns.

The scientists also read with fascination newly arrived translated Chinese pictorial schoolbooks describing how animals behave before earthquakes:

Cattle, sheep, mules and horses do not enter corrals; rats move their homes and flee, hibernating snakes leave their burrows early, frightened pigeons continuously fly and do

not return to nests. Rabbits raise their ears, jump aimless-
ly and bump things. Fish are frightened, jump above
water surface. Every family and every household joins in
observation. The people's war against earthquakes must
be won.

However, in spite of all these reports, the most promising evidence to date of animals predicting earthquakes is the
behavior of the Stanford chimpanzees. Although experts
have no clue as to what physical changes the chimps might be
sensing before the earth moves, they are nonetheless making
even more comprehensive observations of their chimpanzees'
behavior. They are persuaded that other and cheaper animals
should be begin being utilized as monitors in earthquake-
prone regions. As one scientist expressed recently, "I'd be
particularly interested in studying milk and egg production
among cows and chickens because changes in production
levels might tell us right away that another earthquake is
coming.

The Work of UNESCO'S Division of Earth Sciences

In 1964, the United Nations, under the supervision of
UNESCO's Division of Earth Sciences, sponsored the first
intergovernmental conference on earthquakes. After three
weeks of discussions, seminars, and debates, the conference
adopted over 40 resolutions on technical matters whose final
implementation required many years of effort. In spite of
each nation's financial stringency, many international cooperative accomplishments were achieved. For example,
UNESCO supervised the creation of:

• International Seismological Center in the United Kingdom
which uses one of the world's fastest computers to process
data coming into it from observatories across the globe, and

from this information to produce monthly earthquake bulletins.

• Regional Seismological Center for South America in Lima, Peru, which acts as a link between the national seismological services and also coordinates regional studies of seismicity and earthquake risk.

• International Institute of Seismology and Earthquake Engineering (Tokyo) which since 1964 has trained more than 200 scientists and engineers.

• Survey Office for the Seismicity of the Balkan Region which brought together seismologists, geologists, and engineers from five countries in a pioneering effort to define seismic risk on a regional basis in terms directly applicable to earthquake resistant design and construction.

• Installation network of modern, uniform seismographs in four nations of Southeast Asia and the training of scientific and technical personnel to operate the network.

• Institute of Earthquake Engineering and Engineering Seismology at the University of Skopje, Yugoslavia, a center which has become one of the leading centers of training and research in the field.

• And, the large scale research program in soil dynamics at the National University of Mexico, concerned particularly with the design of foundations for buildings in earthquake zones.

Several of these achievements depended upon financial support from the UN Development Program. While progress has been slow, it has nonetheless been steady and may be expected to continue despite financial uncertainities.

The Earthquake Prediction Council

In what appears to be a small step toward solving a major problem, the U.S. Geological Survey designated a team of scientists at its Menlo Park, California, facility as the nation's first Earthquake Prediction Council. The council will coordinate additional research in the field of earthquake prediction and eventually make recommendations to its superiors as to whether scientific readings warrant issuing an official earthquake prediction. Geological Survey director Dr. V. E. McKelvey said the council "marks a major step toward the development of a system for the orderly and effective issuance of earthquake predictions," but he was quick to note that such predictions are currently not possible. "Nevertheless," McKelvey adds, "such a capability is possible in the near future because of important progress in earthquake research." He said scientists are using instruments to detect certain geophysical signs that can be interpreted to forecast an earthquake, and added he is optimistic "about reaching the long-sought goal of prediction."

California's New Strong-Motion Instrumentation Program

In order to gather vitally needed information on the nature of active faults in California, in 1971 the state legislature enacted, and the governor signed into law, Chapter 8 of Division 2 of the Public Resources Code (SB No. 1374), to establish, develop, and regulate a statewide strong-motion seismograph instrumentation program. A strong-motion seismograph (also called an accelerograph) is an instrument designed to record the stronger vibrations caused by earthquakes. It does not record weaker vibrations, during which it remains in a passive state, but produces records only when a potentially or actually damaging earthquake takes place nearby and triggers the instrument. The type of seismograph used for recording most earthquakes is too sensitive for this use; it is driven "off-scale" by the very earthquake the strong-motion instrument records.

One section of the new law states that "It is the intent of the legislature to provide adequate instrumentation throughout California." This indicates that instrumentation is presently inadequate.

Until the San Fernando earthquake occurred, out of a total of 100 strong-motion records, we had only about 10 strong-motion recordings that were at all useful in designing structures to be earthquake resistant. Strong-motion accelerographs were not developed until 1932 and even as recently as 1969 there were only some 300 instruments distributed throughout the state. Since then the Seismological Field Survey of the National Oceanic and Atmospheric Administration cooperating with numerous other organizations, has increased the number of installations until there are now more than 500 instruments throughout the state. Nearly half of these instruments are in Los Angeles as a result of a 1965 city ordinance requiring three accelerographs in each building over six stories in height. The other accelerographs are located elsewhere along the California coastal region. In the short period of time that these 500-plus instruments have been installed, there had been few strong motion records obtained until the San Fernando earthquake struck in 1971 to teach us many costly lessons.

It is necessary to have accelerographs in various types of structures to tell how those structures behaved during an earthquake. However, presently almost all accelerographs are in tall buildings. Although some idea of the ground motion can be determined from records within the buildings, that alone is not enough. It is vitally important that there also be instruments located on soil and rock formations so that the ground motion recorded may be studied and considered in construction design and land use decisions.

The disastrous San Fernando earthquake provided an

abundance of valuable information from accelerographs. We have far more usable records now than in all previous years. But very few instruments were in the San Fernando area where most of the damage occurred; 90 percent were in downtown Los Angeles where damage was minor, and we are still lacking data on the characteristics of the most damaging motions. Only two instruments were located on the ground in areas not influenced by building motion. Currently, instruments are being placed in geographic areas not yet covered; on representative soil and rock sites throughout the state, and on a broad group of representative buildings and structures.

One of the problems in a number of California cities is that no present ordinance requires strong-motion instruments in low buildings or on the ground. Yet, most earthquake injuries and deaths have occurred in buildings less than six stories in height. Some smaller communities and lightly populated areas do not have strong-motion instruments, yet these may be the very areas that will provide critical knowledge to help protect not only the area itself, but heavily populated areas miles away.

The new law requires that all counties and cities shall collect a fee from all applicants for building permits which will be based on the building department permit valuation. This amounts to only a few cents per $1,000 worth of construction—not a great deal to pay for information that may ultimately save many lives and protect against great financial losses.

Earthquake Prediction and Public Policy

A Panel on the Public Policy Implications of Earthquake Prediction, working under the Advisory Committee on Emergency Planning, was established by the National Academy of Sciences of the National Research Council in April of 1974. That panel was mandated to provide advice to the Federal Disaster Assistance Administration of the Department of Housing and Urban Development that would serve as a basis for the formulation of public policy relating to an expected earthquake prediction capability. The types of governmental response with which the panel was concerned included warning of public officials and of the general public; governmental actions to mitigate the loss of life and property; and the need for further studies and research. The panel's responsibilities complemented those of the Panel on Earthquake Prediction which was conducting a state-of-the-art assessment of the physical science aspects of earthquake prediction. The panel's report was intended for use by decision-makers in federal, state, and local governments and in private agencies, by leaders in the business community and other parts of the private sector, by scientists and engineers concerned with disaster prevention, mitigation, and preparedness, and by interested citizens.

The conclusions and recommendations of that panel are as follows:

• The highest priority should be given to earthquake prediction and the saving of lives, with secondary attention given to minimizing social and economic disruption and property loss, provided that the costs for earthquake prediction are within the limits society is willing to accept.

• Earthquake prediction should be used in conjunction with a complete program of earthquake hazard reduction, and not as a substitute for any of the procedures in current use.

• Research has to be undertaken that will monitor responses to the actual *predictions* of moderate and major earthquakes. The plan should include a comprehensive examination of the social, economic, legal, and political effects of the prediction and of the actual quake.

• The primary responsibility for planning and responding to earthquake predictions should be assigned to federal, state, local, and private agencies having broad concern for community and economic planning and for disaster preparedness and response, rather than to newly formed agencies established especially to deal with earthquake prediction and warning, or to agencies concerned primarily with emergency response.

• A public agency should be assigned the responsibility to (1) identify groups of people most likely to need special assistance in the event of an earthquake or to suffer disproportionate loss and disruption when an earthquake is predicted; (2) develop a plan to offset, insofar as is practicable, the inequitable costs and suffering attendant on both the quake and the prediction; (3) help unorganized population segments to recognize how the earthquake prediction affects their interests.

• A comprehensive study should be launched on the legal problems likely to be encountered as earthquake prediction capabilities develop. Preparation of a compendium of federal and state laws pertaining to earthquake prediction and earthquake mitigation measures would be a useful beginning.

• Predictions should be developed, assessed, and issued to the public by scientists rather than by political officials. Procedures must be developed to ensure the free and timely flow of information concerning predictions to all segments of the public. Legislation may be required to assure that the information that an earthquake will occur at a given location and time will not be withheld from general knowledge to the advantage of special interests.

• A designated federal agency should establish a group of governmental and non-governmental scientists who can be called upon to evaluate specific earthquake predictions. The responsibility for establishing this group should not be vested in any agency that is involved in the technical pursuit of earthquake prediction. This agency should also maintain a public record of all published predictions.

• A designated federal agency should confer promptly with governors of the principal earthquake-prone states or their representatives to clarify the respective responsibilities of each level of government and to establish procedures of issuing earthquake warnings.

• A warning should be issued by elected officials promptly after a credible prediction of a potentially destructive earthquake has been authenticated. A warning should include a frank assessment of the prediction, noting the possibilities for error, information on the types and extent of damage that the earthquake could cause, a statement concerning plans being developed to prepare for the quake, and advice concerning appropriate action to be taken by individuals and organizations.

• Careful attention should be paid to the problems of communicating to segments of the population that might otherwise only receive last-minute warnings belatedly. These segments include such groups as foreign-speaking minorities, the physically handicapped, tourists, and the socially isolated.

• Each threatened community should examine the applicability of each of the following major kinds of hazard- reduction measures: (1) evacuating limited areas and vacating dangerous structures; (2) accelerating structural-design and maintenance programs; (3) employing land-use planning and management powers in relation to the predicted locale of the quake; (4) protecting essential natural gas and other community lifelines; (5) dealing with such possible hazards as nuclear plants, vulnerable dams, highly flammable structures and natural cover, and facilities involving the risk of explosion or the release of dangerous chemicals.

• It should be accepted policy on the part of the public and private agencies that a considerable part of the financial assistance normally available to a community after an earthquake should be made available as needed for hazard-reduction measures taken in response to an authenticated prediction of a potentially destructive earthquake.

• Emergency plans should include programs for broad and active citizen involvement in preparing for the earthquake.

• Upon issuance of an earthquake warning a joint governmental and private sector commission should be established to monitor the economy in the threatened areas to ensure early detection of changes, and make recommendations to the government, business, and labor organizations as needed. Representatives of insurance and investment organizations should be included and should play an integral part in the work of the commission.

• In the event of a credible earthquake prediction, policymakers must continuously weigh the relative merits of sustaining the economy in the threatened area at its pre-warning level or of encouraging some orderly outflow of capital. Economic subsidies may be required either to sustain the economy or to protect groups of people who would otherwise suffer hardship as a consequence of economic dislocation resulting from the prediction and warning.

• Consideration should be given to the development of standards to govern the practices of businesses and individuals offering services to the public regarding earthquake mitigation.

• Research is needed on the probable decisions affecting the economy of the threatened areas made by both local and national business and financial leaders and the various economic interactions that are likely to result from these decisions.

• And, finally, the likely effects of earthquake predictions on how various kinds of markets process information and discount changes in the size and timing of losses should be studied in depth. Special attention should be focused on markets for securities (private and public), land markets, financial institutions, insurance practices, metropolitan and local public finance, and problems of financing and maintaining public utility operation.

Man-Made Earthquakes

A major development that has greatly increased the understanding of earthquake mechanisms is the documentation of man-made earthquakes.

The first clue came in 1945 when a scientist documented approximately 600 local tremors during the 10 years following the formation of Lake Mead in Arizona and Nevada. Since then it has been found that the filling of other reservoirs has been accompanied by tremors.

In 1966 another researcher demonstrated a correlation between the rate of injection of waste fluids and the frequency of earthquakes in the vicinity of the Rocky Mountain Arsenal well near Denver. A similar correlation was found at the Rangely oil field in northwestern Colorado, the site of a secondary recovery operation involving the injection of water under pressure.

Similarly, underground nuclear explosions in Nevada have caused numerous small earthquakes close to the test sites.

In addition to providing new insight into the mechanisms of earthquakes, these discoveries provide a potential means for modifying or controlling them. In some cases fluid injections or small explosions may gradually release built-up strain in a series of minor, harmless quakes. Conversely, in regions where high subterranean pore pressure increases the danger of quakes, as when reservoirs are filled, extraction of fluids could act as a safety valve. A U.S. Geological Survey project now underway at Rangely uses pumps at four wells to reduce fluid pressure in the earthquake focal region.

Some scientists believe that what remains to be done in California is to estimate how near the breaking point the San Andreas fault is. One way to find out, they say, is to inject fluids into an area under very controlled conditions and increase the pressure just to the point where tiny tremors occur. The researchers could then extrapolate to find the amount of stress needed to trigger a major quake. The recurrence interval for the San Andreas fault, they believe, can be estimated as anywhere from 200 to 50 years. The last major quake along the fault was in 1906. So, on the basis of present knowledge, we can't say for sure whether the next major quake is overdue or we have more than 100 years to wait.

New Evidence Links Dams to Earthquakes

Recently, two government geologists have found disturbing evidence that high dams back up enough water to trigger earthquakes which could damage or destroy the dams. Desiree Stuart-Alexander and Robert Mark of the U.S. Geological Survey in Menlo Park reported that detailed earthquake information gathered by other scientists throughout the world showed a definite correlation between the depth of water behind high dams and the frequency of earthquakes in the immediate areas of 19 dams ranging from 150 to 250 meters in height. Five have been shaken by earthquakes greater than 3.0 on the Richter scale.

Included in this data was the August 1, 1975, earthquake which heavily damaged Oroville, California. This city is situated below the huge earthen Oroville Dam on the Feather River. Scientists are not certain whether the Oroville temblor was triggered by the dam completed in 1968.

The shock, which registered 6.1 on a fault long considered inactive, sparked widespread interest in the relationship between quakes and artificial lakes. There are two prevailing theories about the effect of millions of tons of water on areas where earthquakes have occurred. One, involving so-called fault loading, theorizes that the weight of the water exerts massive pressure on the fault, causing it to shift, thereby creating an earthquake.

The other is based on the effects of water being forced into the pores of rocks beneath reservoirs. Geologists have known for a long time that saturated rock has less strength than dry rock. As rocks locked in place for millions of years weaken, shaking may occur.

The Stuart-Alexander and Mark study illustrated that five earthquakes were observed worldwide near 78 dams between 90 and 120 meters high—an incidence of 6 percent. This increased to 17 percent among dams from 120 to 150 meters high. But a number of earthquake scientists were critical of the report. They contend that it does not take into account so called "background seismicity" of quakes that would occur regardless of dams being built. They argue that the places you build high dams are also places where there are often earthquakes and the report could lead to the assumption that quakes will occur near high dams. In their defense, Stuart-Alexander and Mark argued that they simply compiled a collection of data on past temblors. Will Peak, chief geologists for the California Division of Safety of Dams, praised the report as an excellent source of hitherto uncorrelated information.

But many earth scientists believe that reservoirs indeed trigger earthquakes. In Japan, one of the most seismically active regions in the world, scientists are considering a recommendation of lowering dams or moving people away from them. Said one Japanese scientist, "It's not research statistics we're after. We're talking about the safety of people."

Thus, in California, as in other parts of the United States, earthquakes near high dams will come under more intensive study. Although a causal link is not certain, the question poses serious implications for dam projects under consideration.

H-Bombs For Earthquakes

If a temblor strikes a populated area, roads may be torn up, buildings toppled, and untold lives lost. Such destructive force seems as devastating as a man-made nuclear blast. Fascinated by the awesome similarity, some seismologists have proposed using the power of the atom to tame the mighty rumbles of the earth. Nuclear detonations at strategic locations far below the surface could be used to keep earthquakes under control. The theory is based on the inherent characteristics of quakes. Although their science is still in its infancy, seismologists know that earthquakes are caused by gradual shifts of the earth's crust. As long as such movements are small and unimpeded, there is little danger of a quake. But strains inevitably build up along the fault line—the zone where the crust has moved from the rock adjacent to it. If these pressures become great enough, the crust suddenly breaks loose again, lurches violently and sends out shock waves in all directions.

Seismologists now argue that nuclear devices might relieve the stresses before they go on the rampage. Exploded two to three miles underground at intervals of 12 to 30 miles along a fault zone, the bombs would set off a series of relatively small shocks. Properly timed, these jolts would jog along the crust ever so slightly to release the forces working against it. The blasts would in effect be seismic safety valves, letting off small but significant amounts of pressure whenever an earthquake threatened.

The idea presents enormous difficulties. Seismologists would have to know exactly where and when to explode the bombs—an art that still eludes them, although they may eventually be able to predict quakes by carefully calculating earth stresses. Still more delicate would be the decision on the size of the bomb. Scientists say that the job probably could be done by high-yield nuclear devices of one to ten megatons, presumably H-bombs. But other seismologists point out that an explosion meant only to keep the earth's crust moving slightly may, in fact, make it lurch violently and actually precipitate a major quake.

The chances are small, but not zero. Some scientists think that a less dangerous method of earthquake control might be to pump liquid into a fault region. Such fluids would relieve stresses by acting, in part, as underground lubricants. Yet this method also poses dangers. During late 1969, recent shocks were apparently triggered in the Denver area by the disposal of chemical wastes in deep underground wells.

In defense of their scheme, the scientists point to the studies of seismic effects of underground nuclear tests staged by the Atomic Energy Commission in Nevada, a highly quake-prone region. Though each blast was followed by countless small aftershocks, none reached quake proportions and all were substantially weaker than the original explosion. The AEC is convinced that there is little risk in conducting such tests. It has already detonated a 1.2 megaton H-bomb on Amchitka Island in the Aleutians, another major quake zone. To the dismay of scientists, however, these explosions were designed by the AEC not for such peaceful purposes, as quake control, but only to test new military weapons.

Social Implications

There is little question that successful earthquake predictions can lead to a great reduction in loss of life, property damage, greater safety for dams and nuclear reactors, as well as to a more rapid restoration to normal living after the shock. But obviously little social benefit can result from earthquake predictions regardless of how accurate and precise they are unless careful planning takes place in response to the predictions.

For a long time to come, prediction capabilities will depend on relatively dense instrumentation along highly seismic areas. Currently, sites for instrumentation have been chosen more on the basis of seismic activity than of social significance. Consequently, early successful predictions are likely to be for areas of relatively low population density. Eventually, a decision will have to be made about when and where to install instrumentation intended primarily to provide socially useful warnings rather than research data. That decision may be a decade away. Regardless, argue seismologists, such a decision would be inappropriate until the whole warning-and-response system has been carefully thought through and planned.

Because of complex economic and social effects, many a scientist casts a skeptical eye on earthquake predictions. For example, what really would happen in Los Angeles or San Francisco if and when seismologists are finally able to predict oncoming earthquakes reliably?

Garrett Hardin, professor of Human Ecology of the University of California at Santa Barbara, argues "If you knew at the last minute that an earthquake was coming you could take the china off the shelves and pack it in excelsior. But this would make sense only if there was a high probability that the quake would take place soon. With a low probability for an imminent earthquake, little evasive action will be taken. If you pack your china away today because an earthquake will probably occur sometime in the next six months, what do you eat off of in the meantime? The china is only symbolic of a whole class of arrangements that are necessary for normal, sane, everyday living. Unreliable early earthquake warnings would be a veritable sword of Damocles hanging over the head of the citizenry.''

What worries seismologists most, however, is whether earthquake predictions should be released to the public until a formal mechanism has been established for doing so. That is, by what channel should such information be released in order to minimize the effects of earthquakes? Seismologists realize that such predictions cannot be kept secret. Sooner or later, word leaks out. Also, issuing a prediction bulletin to the public places the seismologist's scientific reputation on the line.

In the future, many premature predictions will be made due to the inexactness of the science. Public response to those predictions will likely be very expensive. For example, if the U.S. Geological Survey suddenly announced, ''There is a high probability of a severe earthquake in Piedmont within the next three months,'' who would purchase a home in the city? Who would invest in a local business, or even in the public utilities? Naturally, there would be many residents willing to sell. Many people will quit their jobs and move from the area. Other sales would be required to settle estates. Whatever the causes, the existence of a surplus of sellers would produce a catastrophic drop in real estate values. Panic selling might even extend to the shares of locally based business concerns.

Thus, decisionmakers need guidance about whether and how to respond to an earthquake prediction. Most seismologists feel the best compromise between the scientist's freedom to make his findings public and society's need to be protected from costly responses to false alarms is to form an official body to thoroughly dissect and evaluate such predictions as soon as possible after they are made.* If such a reviewing body concludes that a prediction is not well grounded in evidence, that conclusion reached prior to making a prediction public will save needless social response. Yet, if such a reviewing body should endorse a prediction, appropriate social response would become an urgent task.

With or without such a reviewing body, predictions will undoubtedly be announced over the coming years by competent seismologists and agencies. Thus, earthquake predictions must be accompanied by estimates of confidence level and by sufficient backup data so that their merits can be evaluated. Thinking about the design of operational earthquake warning-and-response systems should begin now, say the seismologists, in time to permit thorough cost-benefit analysis of alternative designs. Such an effort must include seismologists, earthquake engineers, experts on social warning systems, and other social scientists and representatives of the governmental agencies. Then, the system will be able to more efficiently and humanely issue seismological data on a routine basis. Warning categories will probably be small in number. However, they will be explicit, similar to those now used for hurricanes and tornadoes. Thus, earthquake prediction as a scientific achievement can be converted to a useful social tool. Seismologists are the first to point out that earthquake prediction, like all other technological capabilities, can be used well or used poorly. Used intelligently, it holds tremendous potential for saving lives, reducing property damage, and smoothing the transition back to normal post-earthquake living.

In conclusion, then, the first question that will be raised by the average citizen when an earthquake is credibly predicted is "How will this event affect me?" Some studies have been made of the likely effect of an earthquake if it were lo-

---

*Currently, two bodies exist as the possible official body: the U.S. Geological Survey and the California Office of Emergency Preparedness.

cated within a large metropolitan region, and considerable work on predicting earthquake hazards is underway in the overall national hazard reduction program. More work is needed and is planned under the proposed expanded program.

With the possibility of a credible prediction being issued at any moment, several steps have been taken to assure appropriate verification and release of predictions. Under the Disaster Relief Act of 1974 and subsequent delegations of authority, the director of the U.S. Geological Survey was given the responsibility to issue warnings of possible earthquake disasters to state and local officials and to provide technical assistance to these officials to insure that timely and effective disaster warning is provided. The director has formed an Earthquake Prediction Council to advise him on the credibility of predictions that have been formulated and has devised a plan for the issuance of such warnings. The state of California has already formulated its own plan for handling earthquake predictions and formed its own prediction review council. The director of the U.S.G.S formally advised the governor of California on March 17, 1976, that the southern California uplift could be the precursor to one or more large earthquakes, but that at this time there is no evidence to suggest a specific prediction. A meeting was held for public officials in 1975 to begin to discuss appropriate response to earthquake predictions.

Generally public leaders have found little time to respond to this hypothetical problem when they have so many other immediate problems to solve. Nevertheless, since our ability to predict earthquakes is rapidly increasing, considerably more effort is needed in devising appropriate responses of public officials to these predictions. Some responses will need to be made immediately after a prediction is issued when there will not be much time to think.

In 1975, a panel on Public Policy Implications of Earthquake Prediction issued a detailed report. Among their many recommendations, they emphasized that there were many legal questions that should be cleared up prior to the first credible prediction of a damaging earthquake. A primary question is the liability of a person issuing a prediction, issuing a warning as to how to respond to a prediction, or, for example, requesting his or her employees to report for work at the time of a predicted earthquake. Another key question is what powers will federal and local officials have to make funds available in advance of a credibly predicted disater.

A detailed socioeconomic study of the likely effects of an earthquake prediction shows that the first credible prediction with an extended lead time is likely to cause severe local economic depression and social disruption unless responsible public officials and business executives take decisive steps to clarify issues of liability, insurance, financial assistance, and proper communication with the public. Research in these areas needs to be stepped up and is planned under the new national earthquake program. Considerable effort is needed to apply the results of this research at the federal, state and local policy levels. Currently, no such effort is being made.

When the Haicheng earthquake was predicted in China, there appears to have been an orderly response by most of the people. Buildings were evacuated, food and water supplies organized, and movies shown in the town square to keep people occupied. Such an orderly response is not as likely in the U.S. if a similar prediction is issued, since in China there has been an aggressive and widespread education campaign on earthquake hazards, techniques of earthquake prediction, and appropriate responses to a prediction. Local officials had been prepared in advance to provide the necessary emergency actions, temporary shelters, medical supplies and the like. Of course the Chinese people own their industry, farmland, houses, etc., collectively so that liability and insurance are not problems as in the United States Educational programs need to be intensified in the U.S., especially in earthquake prone areas.

VI

Learning How To Save Lives

While scientists attempt credible predictions and gradually improve their precision and accuracy, long-term programs to reduce existing hazards should be accompanied by safety steps providing for the relocation and care of residents who are threatened, for bracing structures, and for curtailing or halting commercial and other activities involving unnecessary risks. Emergency measures should also include advance planning and preparation for rescue and assistance, fire fighting, and similar disaster responses, including post- earthquake recovery measures.

Today, California has an engineering rule of thumb to guide decisionmakers. The rule is that every significant structure can be expected to undergo at least one major earthquake in its lifetime. All should therefore be located, designed, and constructed to withstand future shaking or ground failure. Although every building should be made secure against earthquake shaking, the rule is hard to follow, especially for those older structures with major hazards that will be costly and time-consuming to correct and eliminate. The primary dangers include: (1) old and otherwise hazardous buildings, along with newer ones which may collapse during moderate or great earthquakes, injuring or killing oc-

173

cupants. Death and injuries are commonly caused by toppling chimneys, falling brick from wall facings and roof parapets, collapsing walls, falling ceiling plaster, light fixtures, and pictures. Fires from broken chimneys, broken gas lines, and similar causes may be aggravated by the lack of water due to broken mains. Flying glass from broken windows, overturned bookcases, fixtures and other furniture and appliances are also potentially destructive. Fallen power lines will take their toll, along with the drastic human actions resulting from panic. (2) Dams which may fail catastrophically; (3) landslides, including those which may fall into reservoirs and cause overflow; (4) a number of critical facilities which could be damaged, knocked out of service, or caused to malfunction, so as to endanger substantial populations (e.g., nuclear reactors, plants storing explosives or toxic materials, fire fighting facilities, hospitals, major utilities, and highrise buildings and other structures normally containing large numbers of people).

With respect to hazardous buildings, there is at present no organized state or federal program for reducing or eliminating the dangers posed by many old structures, or by newer structures which may not be sufficiently earthquake resistant.

Currently, California is reviewing the safety of dams for which it is responsible. This activity was stepped up after the San Fernando earthquake of 1971 and the near failure of Van Norman Dam, which endangered a large, populated area. There is no state program for reviewing federally owned dams. Nor is there a state policy for dealing with potential landslides.

The handling of critical facilities is highly varied. Nuclear reactors, for example, are recognized as unusually sensitive, and are subject to strict federal design requirements. But there appears to be no effective regulation or review of the seismic adequacy of most other critical facilities.

A Crucial Objective: Earthquake-Resistant Physical Plants

The best long-term policy is to provide a safe physical plant (e.g., the buildings, bridges, dams, factories, and other physical facilities that people use and depend upon). Consequently, a principal goal should be to make sure that all structures and facilities can withstand severe earthquake shaking without significant casualties to humans and without excessive damage or undue economic losses. In short, except for the emergency measures, most public and private efforts related to earthquake hazard should seek the basic objective of guaranteeing shock-resistant structures in all regions likely to experience damaging earthquakes.

Experts are therefore insisting on the need for good design and planning, regardless of the future success of earthquake prediction. Since prediction cannot prevent earthquakes, good earthquake engineering design in siting and building, as well as appropriate land-use planning, will continue to be indispensable even when a prediction capability exists.

While many agencies have important roles in earthquake safety, the review of overall policy and its effectiveness is the principal job of the California Seismic Safety Commission created in 1974. The commission is now working on a number of safety projects, including the formulation of a new overall state seismic policy needed to reduce risks to acceptable levels. Implementing safety policy will be a major enterprise, requiring better use of existing knowledge, as well as an improved understanding of the nature of the hazard, and of workable ways to reduce it.

The architect who designs structures on or adjacent to active earthquake faults carries a high degree of responsibility upon his shoulders. Often the lives of hundreds of people will depend upon his choice of earthquake-resistant designs and materials. To the general public as well as many seismologists, the matter of engineering principles is of little consequence, because most past and present structures raise few problems. Actually, architects and engineers are not in agreement as to what safe engineering principles or architecture really is.

Many seismologists have been impressed by the flexible yielding and recovery of ordinary light Japanese houses during moderate earthquakes, even though they often fail hopelessly in strong shaking. This concept of flexibility as opposed to rigidity for safe design has persisted for more than 70 years. After the Tokyo earthquake of 1923 most Japanese and foreign engineers were satisfied with the results of the rigid-body principle in designing against lateral accelerations. Nevertheless, a few brave dissenters went so far as to advocate extreme flexibility.

Flexibility and rigidity are obviously artificial extremes. Resistance to earthquakes is fundamentally a problem in motion, not in static equilibrium. In theory, it calls for dynamic design.

G. W. Housner, an early expert in Earthquake-resistant construction, says:

> During an earthquake a structure is excited into a more or less violent vibration, with resulting oscillatory stresses, which depend both upon the ground motion and the physical properties of the structure. This is such a complex dynamic problem that it does not appear feasible to make a precise dynamic stress analysis of the problem, particularly inasmuch as it is not possible to foretell the precise nature of future earthquake ground motion nor to compute precisely all of the physical properties of a structure before it is built. The present methods of design are based upon a static rather than a dynamic approach, the structure being designed to resist certain static lateral forces. The static lateral forces are intended to produce stresses of the same order of magnitude as the maximum dynamic stresses likely to be experienced during an earthquake. Because of the complexity of the vibration problem and the various factors influencing the dynamic behavior of a

structure, it is not possible to state with certainty the correct static loads that should be used in all instances, so that the loads used in present design methods must be considered as approximations which will be improved as additional knowledge is gained.

Seismologists are in basic agreement that flexibility is the key ingredient of any design. They feel that no construction should consist of units, connected or in contact, which respond incoherently to shaking, thereby creating stresses through the connections which would not develop if the units were independent. And, above all, no architectural design should include minor units such as parapets and overhang ornaments inadequately attached.

Frank Lloyd Wright's Flexible Engineering Principles

In the world history of art, there is little question that Frank Lloyd Wright has been the leading force in the development of modern architecture. A genius often mistrusted by those too conventional to follow his logical and imaginative thinking, Wright was endlessly obliged to fight against personal and professional adversities which would have discouraged minor men. Today, almost 20 years after his death, he emerges as the one architect whose vision offers the world an engineering solution which could allow private and commercial structures to withstand and ride out tremendous earthquake shocks.

During this past century, one of the few major buildings to survive an 8.3 Richter scale earthquake near its epicenter was the Imperial Hotel which Frank Lloyd Wright designed for downtown Tokyo during the early 1920s. On September 1, 1923, just a year after the new hotel had been completed, a catastrophic earthquake devastated Tokyo, Yokohama, and surrounding areas. According to official figures, 99,331 people lost their lives. This included 38,000 who were burned to death in an open area of Tokyo where they had congregated, supposedly for safety. Unfortunately, these people were overwhelmed by one of the fiery whirlwinds which often originates in such large conflagrations. During the fire, 128,266 houses were destroyed and an additional 447,128 were burned. To the credit of Frank Lloyd Wright's engineering principle of flexible, organic construction, the Imperial Hotel survived the devastation with only a few cracks. That structure became the main hospital and first aid station within minutes of the disaster since it was the only structure standing for miles around.

Why?

The story is worth telling in some detail.

As early as 1914, a Japanese delegation of business men arrived at Frank Lloyd Wright's home at Taliesin North in Wisconsin, looking for an architect to design their new Imperial Hotel. Recalls Wright,

> They came around the world by way of Europe and on their way to America they heard my name and knew the German publication of my work. They heard the name again and again in Europe and decided to look me up. They saw my buildings and said, 'Well not Japanese, not at all, but will look well in Japan.' Thereupon, I spent six years on studies of earthquake conditions. It never left my consciousness. And we solved the problem of the menace of the quake by concluding that rigidity couldn't be the answer, and that flexibility and resilience must be the answer. So we built the building. It could flex and return to normal. And it did withstand the great quakes.*

In analyzing the nature of the constantly recurring Japanese earthquakes, Wright found them to be of a wave-movement type, not of the sea, but of the earth, ac-

---

*Wright, Frank Lloyd. *An American Architecture*. New York: Horizon Press, 1955. P. 149.

companied by terrific shocks no rigidity could withstand. Arriving in Tokyo in March of 1916 to study the foundation possibilities and hazards of the proposed hotel, he observed rumbling earth noises, frequent shocks, drops in the earth level, and swinging motions. And always with the jarring and swinging and the noises came fire, an even greater hazard. The Japanese had always build lightly and close to the ground, knowing the constant peril of temblors, but this very lightness added to the fire danger. The wood frames and the thin walls of paper were excellent fire materials, so thousands of buildings were often consumed before the fire caused by an earthquake was controlled.

Wright's test borings on the site selected for the hotel showed that it had a crust of about seven feet of earth, but that underneath it was seventy to eighty feet of soft mud, a jelly-like mass that would quiver with every earthquake. Said the architect,

> The soil has the consistency of cheese. And, because of the wave movements, deep foundations like long piles would oscillate and rock the structure. Therefore the foundation should be short or shallow. That mud is a merciful provision—a good cushion to relieve the terrible shocks. Why not float the building upon it, like a battleship floats on salt water. And why not extreme lightness combined with tenuity and flexibility instead of the great weight required by the greatest possible rigidity? Why not, then, a building made as the two hands thrust together palms inward, fingers interlocking and yielding, but resilient to return to original position when distortion ceased? A flexure, flexing and reflexing in any direction. Why fight the quake? Why not sympathize with it and outwit it?*

It was a daring concept, so unorthodox that Wright did not even feel that he could explain it fully to the Japanese

---

Ibid., P. 150.

sponsors of the hotel, one of whom included the Emperor. The Emperor, in fact, was paying 60 percent of the cost, besides furnishing the land.

To test out his ideas, Wright directed the workmen to dig nine-inch holes through the seven-foot crust of earth. Water promptly came up in them, within two feet of the top, and Wright concluded that if concrete were used, it would have to be poured into the holes almost immediately after they were dug. He got tons of pig iron and loaded the test piles, calculating every pound of stone, metal, and furniture that would later be piled on top of them when the hotel was eventually built. He even figured on the "squeeze" that would result on the topsoil when all the piles were in place. Wright's conclusion was that when completed, the hotel and its foundations would sink exactly five inches, which is what actually happened in September of 1923. Another reason why the building would "float" on the marshy surface was that Wright had almost immediately discarded any idea of building a high structure, with the great beams and heavy masonry this would involve. He would use native stone, about as heavy as oak logs, and keep the whole building no more than two stories high.

Frank Lloyd Wright was not in Tokyo when the city was hit by the worst earthquake in her history. However, thirteen days later he received a telegram which vindicated his engineeing principle. It read:

Following wireless received from Tokyo today hotel stands undamaged as monument of your genius hundreds of homeless provided by perfectly maintained service congratulations, signed Okura.

Rather than fight the earth shocks with a rigid type of construction, Wright planned a structure that would "roll with the punch" and yield rather than resist. He built the hotel in sections, like a train, and joined the sections together where they were longer than sixty feet. Floors were a special worry because Wright knew that with ordinary construction, where walls support the floors at their edges, a little rocking of the building tears the floors loose, and they drop. Wright decided that he would cantilever the floors— balance them in the middle, as a waiter balances a tray with his hand under the center.

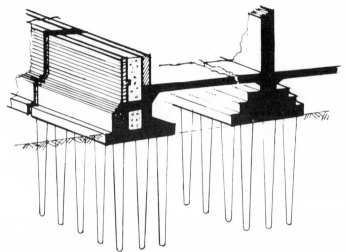

FRANK LLOYD WRIGHT—Imperial Hotel, Tokyo, Japan. Floating foundation on shallow piles in mud strata. Constructed 1922

Wright also knew that in all previous earthquakes the first things to be sheared off by the rocking, grinding, swerving motions were the water pipes and electric lines, resulting in flooding the building or charging it dangerously with electricity. Rather than rigid connections, he decided to put pipes and wires in covered trenches in the basements, away from the foundations, and lead them up to the rooms in vertical pipe shafts. In these shafts the pipes would hang free, yielding and swaying as the building rocked, but not breaking off. Said Wright,

> Roof tiles of Japanese buildings have murdered countless thousands of Japanese in upheavals, so a light, hand-worked green-copper roof was planned. Why kill more?

Although the devastating earthquake of 1923 is the most famous in terms of vindicating Frank Lloyd Wright's system of safe construction, it must be remembered that the Impe-

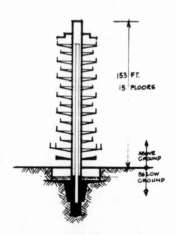

FRANK LLOYD WRIGHT—Johnson Wax Co. Laboratory in Racine, Wisconsin, with cantilevered floors and 'tree' form with "tap-root" foundation. Constructed 1947

rial Hotel also survived the earthquakes of 1927, 1933, 1941, 1944, 1946, 1950, 1952, 1953, 1960, 1962. All had a magnitude of 8.0 or more.

Exactly what is the organic method of construction upon which Wright based his engineering?

To Frank Lloyd Wright, the best example of structure could be found in the great oak tree. Such an oak holds solidly because of its immense deep tap root. Of course, such a genius would never imitate the form of a tree in his own buildings. But Wright understood the principle of structure from the roots anchored in the earth, growing into the trunk with the branches continuing the growth movement by "cantilevering" out. There, the more delicate limbs which sweep out from the branches form into patterns of leaves, which naturally breath and absorb sunlight through this final integrated ornament of nature. Thus, Wright used this same principle with steel, concrete, glass, and every material which came into his scope of thought.

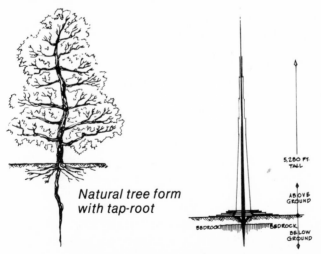

*Natural tree form
with tap-root*

*FRANK LLOYD WRIGHT—"Mile high" building
which incorporates concepts of flexibility and
lightness of structure with "tap-root" foundation.
Designed 1956*

Seismic Engineering Thoughts from a San Francisco Architect

Aaron G. Green, F.A.I.A., a San Francisco architect responsible for several Bay area housing projects, court houses, civic center, and private homes, has followed the tradition of logical and flexible engineering principles.

His thoughts on seismic and architectural hazards are quoted at length because of their relevance for safety:

> Since Frank Lloyd Wright's major structural concepts were proven valid, over the skepticism of the engineering profession, little contribution has been made to further the state of the art of advanced building design to resist seismic action. Structural engineers continue to promote the vast added cost penalties; to design more and more rigidity, mass and weight into buildings instead of tenuity, continuity, flexibility and lightness of structure as espoused and demonstrated in the successful buildings of Wright.
>
> Building forms which reflect the inherent structural integrity found in nature's creations may be synthesized to illustrate many valid basic structural concepts into actual building construction with superior resistance to seismic movement. When the dynamic forces of earthquake propel the building components, the stresses resulting from this energy are proportional to the weight of the mass. Designs now may take advantage of various materials providing lightness and tenuity resulting in added safety with reduced costs. Today's architects and engineers are slow indeed in responding to this design challenge which goes waiting and wanting for lack of courage and creativity. Meanwhile the status quo engineering mentality frightens the populace with dire predictions of earthquake disaster to all buildings, all the time pouring more and more bulk concrete and other weighted factors to add to their fees and heavy construction cost burdens. The dog continues to run in circles in an attempt to catch his tail. More weight to make it "stronger"; make it "stronger" to resist the added weight.

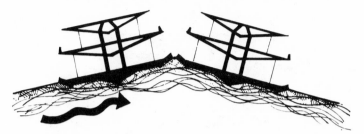

Exaggerated structural diagram showing artic-ulated building components; cantilever principle on floating foundation.

Catenary suspension—Lightweight tensile struc-ture separated from direct contact with earth forces

Sea shells, and similar thin-shell forms found in nature are exemplary prototypes of basic logical structure with inherent continuity and purity of form. Building forms properly inspired by, and related to, such basic pro-totypes, in addition to understanding of the actions of various types of seismic disturbances can be inherently seismic resistant. Such forms may be reduced to distribute stresses throughout the structure, thereby avoiding the build-ups of the great stress magnitude which destroys the traditional structure at its weakest and most brittle points.

System of primary form building—lightweight dome components with flexible interconnecting elements able to withstand undulation

Sea shell form—Basic structure of thin shell patterned on nature's prototype, having lightness of weight and equalization of stresses.

The lightweight structure may have relatively shallow foundations, and as Wright's remarkable Tokyo Imperial Hotel demonstrated, can be said to "ride on the surface" of the earthquake wave motions. Such structures are thereby considerably less involved with sub-surface stresses and more tolerant of less substantial soil characteristics.

Earthquake-Proof Nuclear Reactors

From the time of the first nuclear power plant designs, seismologists have been concerned about the effects strong earthquakes might have upon them. Yet, the structural analysis of nuclear reactor plants is a complicated endeavor involving many assumptions and uncertainities. Today, most earth scientists conclude that the public utilities in cooperation with the federal government are constructing reactor buildings which can resist seismic forces in excess of those anticipated anywhere in the world.

During the 1950s, the first series of research reactors and experimental facilities were built in various parts of the United States, as well as in other nations scattered across the globe. A decade later, that first series was followed by the construction of demonstration power reactors. During that time, the early reactors included consideration of the possible effects of earthquakes upon safety and operability. The approaches to the earthquake problem of early facilities included static analyses of seismic loading, site investigations and earthquake instrumentation, as well as seismic switches. By the late 1950s, dynamic analyses were being made of certain critical systems, reactor fuel elements, cores, piping, and other heavy equipment. Actually, in the early 1960s, the U.S. Atomic Energy Commission authorized a study of nuclear reactors and earthquakes, which was published in 1963.

From this major government document, the first designs of large-scale power plants incorporating seismic analysis were prepared. And, the first major facility in the United States to include a significant emphasis on seismic safety design was the San Onofre Nuclear Generating Station in California. Thus, by the late 1960s, dynamic analysis of nuclear power plant structures and equipment had become ordinary. Site qualification was requiring extensive geological and seismological investigations along with specific regulatory guides concerning seismic design and instrumentation for nuclear power plants. In the late 1960s, the first data resulting from tests on full-scale nuclear power plants were obtained. But during that time, several large-scale nuclear power plants planned for California were cancelled after strenuous objections largely due to seismic unknowns raised by various public interest groups. With the cancellations, the

U.S. Atomic Energy Commission became interested in the seismic design process by authorizing additional studies into earthquake resistant nuclear reactor buildings. Also, international interest increased principally with the encouragement of the Japanese who had initially pioneered the work.

From these efforts, new regulations and design guides followed one another rapidly in the next eight years. The earthquake design basis used for nuclear power plant construction was then escalated rapidly, especially following the San Fernando earthquake.

Today, seismologists generally concur that the seismic design of nuclear power plants has become a rather sophisticated act as well as technique. In fact, from a structural engineering point of view, a nuclear power plant is perhaps the safest structure engineered by man with respect to earthquake excitation. More sophisticated analysis, more expensive engineering time and design conservatism, more quality control and inspection, more high-quality materials and more careful site evaluation go into the seismic design and construction of nuclear power plants than any other structure. Besides requiring tens of thousands of hours of engineering time to perform just the seismic design of a power plant, highly sophisticated computer methods have been developed and are used for analysis and testing of the structures and equipment. Based upon comparisons with the seismic design of conventional structures such as steel-frame, high-rise buildings, it is estimated that the margin of conservatism in nuclear power plant design is ten or more times greater than that of conventional structures.

After the 1971 San Fernando shock, a survey was conducted of nuclear reactor facilities in California, Nevada, and parts of Arizona. It was learned that this western region of the United States had 26 power reactors or research reactors either fully functioning or under construction. Over half of these facilities had built into them strong-motion earthquake instruments, or seismic switches to shut down the reactor during the first shock waves of an earthquake. The remaining nuclear facilities indicated they were in the process of installing them. At the time of the San Fernando tragedy, both the Atomic Energy Commission and the nuclear industry were establishing criteria of seismic instrumentation requirements. Today, all nuclear power plants under construction, or in the process of design, are by federal and state laws required to include seismic instrumentation.

Nuclear Reactor Seismic Instrumentation

From the perspective of the power plant owner, the prime reason for installing and maintaining the instrumentation is to obtain records of ground motion and responses experienced by the plant and safety related structures and equipment.

Following an earthquake, the plant operator will make a decision as to whether the nuclear reactor can operate or should be shut down for inspection and repair. But such a crucial decision does not depend upon seismic instrumentation alone. The decision of whether or not to shut down a nuclear power plant after an earthquake is made after visual inspections as well as consideration of the judgments of the plant supervisor and experts called in. Also, readings from other instrumentation pertaining to the safety condition of the nuclear reactor are analyzed. In the likely event of a small magnitude earthquake, or even a large earthquake occurring miles away, the plant is not shut down unless visible damage has occurred. But the decision to continue operating the plant first requires substantiation with the licensing agencies. This is based upon a recorded ground motion and equipment responses and the analyses made of these records.

Each nuclear reactor location site has been assigned what is termed *Operating Basis Earthquake*. This implies that if indeed an earthquake magnitude is greater than that OBE, the reactor is immediately shut down until studies can be undertaken to determine its safety. Most of western regions OBE's are 8.5. However, seismologists, government, state, and local officials are all in agreement that shutdown criteria have been carefully analyzed and rational, safe policies established. The decision to shut down the plant must incorporate data from many, many sources, not just seismic information.

The Diablo Canyon Controversy

Recently, Dennis Allison, the Federal Nuclear Regulatory Commission's overseer for the Pacific Gas and Electric Company's $1 million dollar nuclear power plant at Diablo Canyon near San Luis Obispo, California described his situation as "urgent, messy, and full of controversy." With the first of two 1,100 megawatt units expected to be completed and operating by July of 1977, the controversy has been fanned by anti-nuclear groups who claim the Hosgri fault, 120 miles long and three miles offshore from the plant, is active.

In the meantime, PG&E was announcing through its monthly newsletter that because of California's 1976-1977 droughts and delays in licensing the plant, electrical shortages or brownouts may occur during the summer. The first unit was expected to provide power equal to all 65 PG&E hydroelectric plants. A few scientists have added to the controversy by insisting that the Hosgri links up with other active faults in central California.

Over the years, the U.S. Geological Survey analyzed the Hosgri fault and identified it as a fault responsible for a 7.23 magnitude earthquake in 1927. PG&E engineers designed the plant to ride out a 6.75 quake. Federal agencies insisted the utility bring the construction specifications up so that it would withstand a 7.5 shock. Those modifications included added protection for wiring and piping and better shock protection for valves and various kinds of equipment.

When in full operation, the double-domed nuclear plant would add a total of 15 percent to PG&E's capacity. The target date for the second 1,100 megawatt unit is in 1978. To anit-nuclear power advocates, the main concern is the possibility of simultaneous failure in all the backup systems. Supposedly, this might result in the melting down of the reactor which in turn could release large amounts of radiation into the atmosphere.

While the advocates (Mothers for Peace, Ecology Action, and Scenic Shoreline Preservation Conference) were in court to prevent the plant from opening, the nuclear reactor's chief and civil engineers were telling the public that they would not hesitate to have their families stand alongside of them in the operating room during a 7.5 quake.

What the Average Citizen Can Do

There are many safety precautions the average citizen can take to reduce the dangers from earthquakes. For example, before an earthquake even occurs, support local safe buildings codes which provide structures with flexible and earthquake-proof materials. If no such regulations exist in your community, propose and support their enactment. Also, support school building programs which provide for the strengthening of pre-1933 school buildings, or their replacement with earthquake-resistive structures on ground reasonably safe from failure. Join community efforts to insure that cornices, parapets, and other loose objects on building exteriors be removed or securely fastened. Another crucial role a citizen can play is to organize and support emergency programs to prepare for future earthquakes. Indeed, schools and civic organizations can provide a very beneficial service by holding earthquake drills and training sessions. And, the interested and committed citizen can support research of local earthquake problems in order to supply information needed for the siting, design, and construction of new structures.

As a homeowner or tenant, check your own home or apartment for earthquake hazards. Bolt down or provide other strong support for water heaters and other gas appliances since fire damage can result from broken gas lines and appliance connections. Use flexible connections wherever possible, and place large and heavy objects on lower shelves. Shelves can be securely fastened to walls, as can high or top-heavy objects.

In your own new construction and alterations, follow building codes to minimize earthquake hazards. Sites for construction should be selected and engineered to reduce the hazard of damage from an earthquake.

Also, hold occasional home earthquake drills to provide the family with the knowledge to avoid injury and panic during an earthquake. For example, among the crucial instructions is where an operable flashlight can be found. Teach responsible members of your family how to turn off electricity, gas, and water at main switches and valves. Further, check with your local utilities office for instruction.

The citizen can provide for responsible family members to receive basic first-aid training since medical facilities may be overloaded immediately after a severe shock. Call your local Red Cross or civil defense director for information about classes. Also, keep extra flashlights and battery-powered transistor radios in your home, ready for use at all times. Keep immunizations up to date for all family members and conduct calm family discussions about earthquakes and other possible disasters. Above all, be sensitive about what you must do if an earthquake strikes when you are at home. Such planning may enable you to act calmly and constructively in an emergency.

For example, during an earthquake you must remain calm and think through the consequences of any action you take, hopefully calming and reassuring others. If indoors, watch for falling plaster, bricks, light fixtures, and other objects. High bookcases, china cabinets, shelves, and other furniture might slide or topple down, crushing unsuspecting victims. Stay away from windows, mirrors, and chimneys. If in danger, stand in a strong doorway, get under a table, desk, or bed. Usually, it is best not to run outside. If in a high-rise office building, get under a desk. Do not dash for exits, since stairways may be broken and jammed with people. Power for elevators may fail. If in a crowded store, you should not rush for a doorway since hundreds may have the same idea. If you must leave the building, choose an exit as carefully as possible. If outside, avoid high buildings, walls, power poles, and other objects which could fall. You should not run through the streets. If possible, move to an open area away from all hazards. If in an automobile, stop in the safest place available, preferably in an open area.

After an earthquake, you should check for injuries in your family and neighborhood. You should not attempt to move seriously injured persons unless they are in immediate danger of further injury. Check immediately for fires or fire hazards, wearing shoes near debris or broken glass. Check utility lines and appliances for damage. If gas leaks exist, shut off the main gas valve. All electrical power should be turned off if there is damage to house wiring, and a call made to the appropriate utility company in order to report the situation and receive instructions. Above all, do not use matches, lighters, or open flame appliances until you are sure no gas leak exists. Electrical switches or appliances should not be operated if gas leaks are suspected. This creates sparks which can ignite gas from broken lines. No one should touch downed power lines or objects touched by the downed wires. Spilled medicines, drugs, and other potentially harmful materials must be immediately cleaned up. If water is off, emergency water may be obtained from water heaters, toilet tanks, melted ice cubes, and canned vegetables. Someone should check to see that sewage lines are intact before permitting continued flushing of toilets. People should not eat or drink anything from open containers near shattered glass. Liquids may be strained through a clean handkerchief or cloth if danger of glass contamination exists. If power is off, the head of a family should check the freezer and plan meals to use up foods which will spoil quickly. You should use outdoor charcoal broilers for emergency cooking. Telephones should not be used except for genuine emergency calls. Radios must constantly be tuned in for damage reports and information. Chimneys must be checked over their entire length for cracks and damage, particularly in the attic and at the roof line. Unnoticed damage could lead to fire. Approach to chimneys should be made with caution, while the initial check is made from a distance. Closets and storage shelf areas should also be checked. A person should open closet and cupboard doors carefully and watch for objects falling from shelves.

Above all, rumors should not be spread since they often do great harm. No one should go sightseeing immediately, particularly in beach and waterfront areas where seismic sea waves could strike. If possible, people should help in keeping streets clear for passage of emergency vehicles. And, everyone should be prepared for additional earthquake shocks. Although most of these will be smaller than the main shock, some may be larger, or at least enough to cause further deaths and damage.

Everyone should respond to requests for help from police, fire fighters, civil defense, and relief organizations, but not go into damaged areas unless help has been requested. Complete cooperation must be given to public safety officials. In some areas, people may actually be arrested for getting in the way of disaster operations.

Of course, there are no specific rules or formulas which can eliminate all earthquake danger. However, damage and injury can be greatly reduced by following the simple rules outlined above.

Conclusion

In 1976, over 700,000 people died in earthquakes around the globe. In all likelihood, it was the worst year in modern times for earthquake fatalities since 1923, when Tokyo experienced her devastating shock. But, 1556 was the worst year in history when over 800,000 died in central China.

In spite of the huge loss of life in 1976, it was a normal year. Only 15 earthquakes measuring 7.0 or more were experienced. Throughout history, the average has been only 18 quakes with such a high magnitude. As bad luck would have it, however, the 15 earthquakes were close to large population centers where deaths numbered 22,000 in Guatemala, 1,000 in northern Italy, 6,000 in New Guinea, 1,000 in Indonesia, 650,000 in China, 8,000 in the Philippines, and possibly 5,000 more in Turkey.

There is no doubt that seismologists will be able to predict an earthquake of at least a magnitude 7 in California within the next decade, in such a scientifically sound way and with sufficiently small space and time uncertainty as to insure public acceptance and effective response. Programs of routine announcement of reliable predictions will soon follow as naturally as weather reports.

In spite of such incredible advances, there are nonetheless many gaps and unanswered questions in the seismologists' understanding of earthquake phenomena. For example, exactly how does the earth's crust behave before, during, and after an earthquake? How large are the stresses responsible for major earthquakes? Specifically, how do the physical and chemical properties of the inhomogeneous crustal rocks change under stress in the earth?

Perhaps the two most important questions among the unresolved problems of earthquake phenomena are: (1) Will well-identified precursory phenomena indeed forecast imminent shocks? (2) For all the various precursory phenomena, how large and of what character must deviation from base level values be before they can be regarded as true signals of an impending earthquake?

Questions concerning earthquake control are likely to be farther in the future than prediction. Nonetheless, prediction permitting identification of regions in which studies could be made on the feasibility of earthquake control by fluid injection or other means can be developed. Earthquake-control experiments have been successfully achieved on a small scale in the shallow oil field at Rangely, Colorado.

Before earthquake control can become a reality, much more must be known about the physical processes involved, including the magnitude of the stresses, permeability and porosity of rocks, and variations of fluid pressure along fault zones. The Rangely results, coupled with various laboratory studies currently under way, are adding to the capabilities of seismologists to modify and control at least some types of earthquakes.

The prognosis for the future of earthquake prediction and control depends upon the extent of America's commitment to a national program. More studies are urgently needed in more representative tectonic regions to fully explore the feasibility of earthquake control.

The level of financial support and size of the program, insist the earth scientists, must be consistent with the magnitude of the task and the available trained manpower. In order to take the most significant steps in the shortest possible time, the various types of expertise from universities, private industry, and various federal and state agencies should be applied to earthquake prediction and control. Most seismologists argue for a ten-year commitment including five times the current annual federal funding of $10,637,000.*

---

*The total 1976 Congressional budget related to earthquake prediction was:

National Science Foundation	$ 1,700,000
National Science Foundation— Earth Sciences	2,552,000

To put this expenditure into perspective, it has been estimated that a major earthquake today in either San Francisco or Los Angeles could not only claim more than 10,000 lives, but also cause damage exceeding $15 million.

Realizing that a single earthquake may cost a nation more than its national budget and set its economic progress back by five years, Japan, Russia, and China have established major programs of earthquake prediction and hazard reduction. It is now time that America make a national commitment to an effective earthquake prediction-and-response program, and to allocate the necessary resources for the task.

No one should forget that slow but inexorable movements of the crust driven by forces deep within the earth have been going on since our planet was formed and will continue for thousands of millions of years in the future. They are part of the "life process" of the earth by which the crust is constantly renewed and is responsible for formation of the minerals upon which our societies are based.

The instantaneous destruction and loss of life caused by earthquakes can be compared only with that inflicted by a nuclear war. For too long, Americans have assumed people must die in earthquakes. Today, say seismologists, we can live and ride them out, learning more than ever before about our tormented planet in the process.

U.S. Nuclear Regulatory Commission	85,000
U.S. Geological Survey	5,000,000
National Aeronautics and Space Administration	1,300,000
	$10,637,000

In contrast, the People's Republic of China spends $100 million on prediction efforts alone.

A Portfolio of Photographs

San Francisco, April 18, 1906

The 1906 San Francisco earthquake probably had a magnitude of 8.5 on the Richter scale. The San Andreas fault rupture extended some 190 miles from San Juan Bautista near Hollister to Point Arena where it continued under the Pacific Ocean. The average horizontal fault displacement was about 10 feet, although in some places it reached 21 feet. The closest breakage to San Francisco was 1½ miles from the city limits. The financial and commercial centers were approximately 10 miles from the fault rupture.

The loss of life was well over 700, with the bulk occurring in the downtown area. At the time, San Francisco had a population of 400,000. Property damage was approximately $105,008,480. In 1907, the Chamber of Commerce used extrapolated insurance data to derive a loss closer to $350 million for all the structures and their contents. Added to this, of course, one would have to add economic losses from trade and transportation disruptions in lost months, if not years. Some seimologists feel $1 billion is a more accurate projection of real loss.

The three-day conflagration caused more damage than

199

the earthquake. The area of the burned district covered 4.7 square miles, comprising 521 blocks of which 510 were burned. The three main water conduits from storage reservoirs were damaged or destroyed where they crossed over the San Andreas fault. With the collapse of hundreds of pipes along the city's distribution system, coupled with the thousands of service pipes, conflagrations spread without resistance.

This earthquake marked the largest test to date of the new, multistory steel frame buildings. A total of 17 structures ranging in height from 8 to 19 stories experienced the shaking. Extensive nonstructural earthquake damage occurred with sheared bolts, bent I-beams, torn gusset plates, and the like. But none of these multistory buildings was so heavily damaged as to be unsafe.

San Fernando, February 9, 1971

Far better data on life loss, injuries, and property damage are available for this disaster than for any other American earthquake. Some 58 people were killed out of a population of 7,032,000. The collapses at the Veteran's Hospital in the foothills of San Fernando Valley claimed 41 lives, while 6 others died as a result of injuries in the hospital. The total loss to buildings and structures has been estimated at $478.5 million. The tragedy could have been much greater had the nearby Van Norman Dam collapsed, pouring millions of cubic feet of water into the low-lying residential areas. Occurring at 6:01 A.M. most people were still in their wood frame homes which absorbed the shock's intensity very well. Had the quake occurred at 2:00 P.M., or 4:30 P.M., the peak of the evening commute rush hour, thousands of people might have lost their lives.

Prince William Sound, Alaska, March 27, 1964

The 8.4 Richter magnitude earthquake which hit Alaska on Good Friday was slightly greater than the 1906 San Francisco shock. But virtually all the deaths and devastation in this case resulted from tsunami—seismic sea waves. Of the 110 deaths, only 15 resulted during the collapse of a building. The major landslides which resulted in extensive property damage will more than likely occur in San Francisco when the next big quake hits, although seismic sea waves offer no threat. But, once again, a key lesson was learned. Ground shaking does not kill people. It is the collapse of man-made structures such as buildings and dams which creates casualties during severe ground shaking. During this Alaska quake, modern precast concrete performed poorly when compared with other construction materials. Undoubtedly, similar problems will occur in California on a much greater scale in the event of a maximum credible earthquake on a major fault.

Fukui, Japan, 1948

While no unusual surface faulting occurred during this earthquake, important data were obtained for seismologists. The magnitude was 7.3 and over 80 percent of all structures were demolished. Some 5,000 people were killed. But for the first time, cracks and pressure ridges were found which definitely suggested tectonic significance. Also, an unusual characteristic of the tragedy was the opening of large fissures in the alluvium.

Turkey

Northern Turkey has one of the most active earthquake faults in the world. Loss of life during the past century has numbered in the hundreds of thousands, to say nothing of the millions of dwellings destroyed. When a major earthquake strikes during the winter, it leaves large homeless populations exposed to snow and severe colds. Although fault traces have been mapped and fissures and strike-slips are clearly evident, the government has little control over where the peasant population builds. Epicenters for these earthquakes generally occur near the Black Sea where the continuous tectonic line is most active. Because aftershocks are more frequent in this area than in any other area in the world, a theory has been suggested that progressive deterioration is occurring all along the line.

In the following photographs taken in 1966, some 11,000 people lost their lives, primarily crushed under the heavy rock walls of homes and other structures.

The San Andreas Fault

Earth scientists now know that the San Andreas fault system (along with all its earthquakes) is part of a global grid of faults, chains of volcanoes and mountains, rifts in the ocean floor, and deep oceanic trenches which represent the boundaries between the huge shifting plates that make up the earth's lithosphere.

The following series of photographs clearly illustrate the fault line which is moving westward between 1½ and 2½ inches a year. Thus, clearly visible offsets can be seen.

The trend of the San Andreas fault system is roughly northwest-southeast from San Francisco to the south end of the San Joaquin Valley and again from the north of the Salton Sea depressions to the Mexican border.

During the 43-year period between 1934 and 1977, there were more than 8,800 earthquakes with a Richter magnitude of 4 or greater along the fault.

In short, the San Andreas fault cutting through California forms part of the boundary between the Pacific Plate and the North American Plate. Although these plates are moving steadily, the two sides have a tendency to lock together. When this happens, the energy may be stored for decades until the plates unlock and jump several feet in opposite directions parallel to the fault. Such sudden motions produce earthquakes. Nothing can be done to stop the motion of the plates. Thus, California will always continue to experience earthquakes along the San Andreas fault.

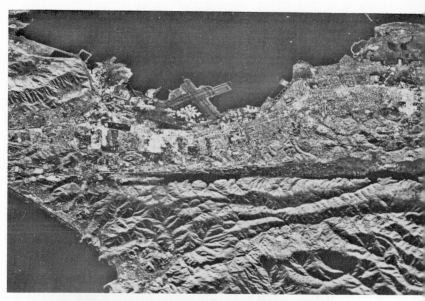

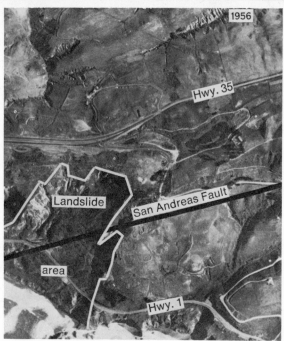

1966

Hwy. 35

Hwy. 1

Landslide area

San Andreas fault

Glossary

Abrasion: The mechanical wear of rock on rock.

Acceleration (high): Motion persisting and forming an appreciable fraction of a whole earthquake disturbance.

Aftershock: Continued shaking after a sizable earthquake. This shock of a major earthquake may be as large as ordinary locally damaging shocks. The epicenters are likely to be distributed over a wide area. A large aftershock may originate closer to a center of population and cause more damage than the main earthquake.

Aftershocks (second order): A series of small aftershocks falling off more rapidly than general aftershock activity.

Airwaves: In an earthquake, these waves are produced directly by the transfer of elastic wave energy from the ground to the air.

Amplification: The increase in earthquake ground motion that may occur to the principal components of seismic waves as they enter and pass through different earth materials.

Asthenosphere: That zone of the solid earth immediately below the lithosphere.

Block tectonics: Areas where shallow earthquakes are frequent due to the relative displacements of blocks separated by large faults which are often nearly straight and dip almost vertically. One such region is California with the basin and range province east of it.

Bore hole: A hole drilled into the earth for exploratory purposes.

Charts (for determining magnitudes): Indentification of phases for deep-focus telesism proceeding usually by trial and error and fitting the readings to charts drawn for various hypocentral depths.

"Circle of Fire": The circum-Pacific belt of active volcano activity. Small scale maps showing active volcanoes and epicenters of large earthquakes illustrate a similar distribution.

Continental shelf: A submerged platform of variable width that forms a fringe around a continent.

Continental shield: Mass of precambrian rock around which a continent has accumulated.

Continental slope: A pronounced slope beyond the seaward margin of a continental shelf.

Compression: External stress applied to an object tending to reduce volume.

Convergent margin: A line along which two plates move toward each other and where old lithosphere is subducted, forced downward into the mantle.

Core (earth's): The innermost zone of the earth. A spherical mass of metallic iron and nickel, 3,488 km in diameter, consisting of a molten outer part approximately 2,128 km thick and a solid inner sphere with a radius of 1,360 km.

Correlation: Determination of equivalence in geologic age and position of the sequences of strata found in two or more different areas.

Creep: The nearly imperceptible slow downslope movement of a plate.

Crust (earth's): The outer part of the lithosphere.

Crust, continental: The earth's crust beneath continents, 20 to 40 km thick, consisting of an upper part having the same elastic properties as sialic rocks and a lower part having the same elastic properties as mafic rocks.

Damping: A resistance to vibration that causes a progressive reduction of motion with time or distance.

Dilatations: The condition of being stretched beyond normal limits.

Dip-slip faulting: Vertical or oblique movement in opposing directions.

Divergent margin: A line along which two adjacent plates move apart from each other and along which new lithosphere is made. Also called a spreading edge.

Earthquake focus: The point of first release of the energy that causes an earthquake.

Epicenter: The point on the earth's surface that lies vertically above the focus of an earthquake.

Fault: A fracture along which the opposite sides have been displaced relative to each other.

Focus: A synonym for hypocenter when writing of deep-focus earthquakes.

Formation: A succession of strata distinctive enough to constitute a basic unit for mapping and description.

Free face: A sloping surface exposed to air or water such that there is little or no resistance to lateral movement of earth materials.

Geodetic measurements: Controls on location (vertical or horizontal) of positions on the earth's surface of a high order of accuracy, usually extended over large areas for surveying and mapping operations.

Geophysical surveys: The use of one or more techniques of physical measurement to explore earth properties and processes.

Gravity (of earth): The inward-acting force with which earth tends to pull all objects toward its center.

Gravity anomaly: The deviation of the observed acceleration of gravity (negative when smaller, positive when larger) from an expected value calculated from the general gravitational field of the earth, considering latitude and elevation; correction is usually added to allow for the effects of irregular topography and structure.

Hydrosphere: The earth's discontinuous water envelope, including the oceans, lakes, streams, ground water, snow, and ice.

Hypocenter: The point believed to represent the position of the initial rupture of the rocks, the point on the surface vertically above the epicenter.

Intensity: The degree of shaking at a specified place. This is not based on measurement but is a rating assigned by an experienced observer using a descriptive scale with grades indicated by Roman numerals from I to XII.

Isoseismal (lines): Mapped as boundaries between regions of successive intensity ratings such as IV and V.

Joint: Fracture on which movement has not occurred in a direction parallel to the plane of the fracture.

Left-lateral movement: A generally horizontal movement in which the block across the fault from the observer has moved to the left.

Lithosphere: The outer zone of the solid earth. The lithosphere includes the crust and the upper part of the mantle. The lower boundary of the lithosphere is the low-velocity zone.

m.: Mass

M.: Magnitude.

Macroseismic effects (of earthquakes): Those which can be observed on their large scale in the field without instrumental aid.

Magnitic field (earth's): The magnetic lines of force surrounding the earth.

Magnitude (of an earthquake): Rating of a given earthquake independent of the place of observation; calculated from measurements on seismograph and expressed in ordinary numbers and decimals.

Mantle (earth's): A zone of rocky matter about 2,800 km thick surrounding the earth's core and covered by the thin crust. The mantle occupies about 80% of the total volume of the earth.

Massive rock: Rock that is fairly uniform in appearance and lacks any breakage surfaces.

Meizoseismal area: Areas within the isoseismals of higher intensity.

Metamorphic rock: Rock formed with earth's crust by transformation in the solid state of pre-existing igneous or sedimentary rocks as a result of high temperature, high pressure, or both.

Microearthquake: An earthquake having a magnitude of 2 or less on the Richter scale.

Microseismic effects (of earthquakes): Those which are small-scale and observable only with instruments. Often this noun is used to signify less continuous disturbances in the ground recorded by seismographs.

Mountain chain: An elongate unit consisting of numerous ranges or systems, regardless of similarity in form or equivalence in age.

Mountain range: An elongate series of mountains belonging to a single geologic unit.

Mountain system: A group of ranges similar in general form, structure, and alignment, and presumably owing their origin to the same general causes.

Normal fault: A vertical to steeply inclined fault along which the block above the fault has moved downward relative to the block below.

Oceanic ridge: (Also called mid-ocean ridge and oceanic rise.) A continuous rocky ridge on the ocean floor, many hundred to a few thousand kilometers wide.

Origin time: The instant at which the earthquake event (apart from foreshocks) commences at the hypocenter.

p.: Angular frequency of ground motion.

P.: Seismological shorthand for longitudinal, or compression-rare-factional, waves through the earth.

Parapets: Portions of side walls extending above the roof line. When constructed of unreinforced and unsupported masonry they create a serious earthquake hazard.

Plastic deformation: A permanent change, excluding rupture, in the shape of a solid.

Potential energy: Stored energy waiting to be used.

Remote Sensing: The acquisition of information or measurement of some property of an object by a recording device that is not in physical or intimate contact with the objects under study.

Reverse fault: A steeply to slightly inclined fault in which the block above the fault has moved relatively upward or over the block below the fault.

Right-lateral movement: Generally horizontal movement in which the block across the fault from an observer has moved to the right.

Rock: Any naturally formed, firm, and coherent aggregate or mass of mineral matter that constitutes part of the earth's crust.

Rock cleavage: The property by which a rock breaks into plate-like fragments along flat planes.

Rock cycle: The cyclic movement of rock material, in the course of which rock is created, destroyed, and altered through the operation of internal and external earth processes.

Sand ridges: Low ridges of sand extended along fissures caused by ground cracking and expulsion of water and sand by liquefaction.

S.: Seismological shorthand for transverse or shear waves through the earth.

Sag pond: Enclosed depression, generally occupied by water, formed when movement along a fault has disturbed the surface or subsurface continuity of drainage.

Scarp: A cliff or steep slope formed by a fault, generally by one side moving up relative to the other.

Sea-floor trench: A long, narrow, very deep basin in the sea floor.

Sedimentary rock: Rock formed from sediment by cementation or by other processes acting at ordinary temperatures at or near earth's surface.

Seismic belt: Large tract subject to frequent earthquake shocks.

Seismograph: An instrument which writes a permanent continuous record of earth motion.

Seismometer: Seismograph whose physical constants are known sufficiently for calibration so that actual ground motion may be calculated from the seismogram.

Seismoscope: A device which indicates the occurrence of an earth-quake but does not write a record.

Strain: The deformation of the body in the vicinity of a given point.

Stress: A point in the interior of a body which is determined by the system of forces acting in the vicinity of that point.

Strike-slip fault: Fault in which movement is principally horizon-tal.

T.: Period of ground motion.

Tectonic earthquake: Believed to be associated with faulting or other structural processes. This excludes volcanic earthquakes, as well as minor shocks due to less important causes.

Tectonics: The study of earth's broad structural features.

Teleseism: An earthquake recorded by a seismograph at a great dis-tance. By international convention this distance is required to be over 1,000 kilometers (621 miles) from the epicenter.

Thrust fault (also called a thrust): Low-angle reverse fault with dip generally less than 45°.

Topographic map: A map that delineates surface forms.

Topography: The relief and form of the land.

Transform fault: A special class of strike-slip fault that links major structural features.

Transit time: The elapsed time between the origin time and the ar-rival of a given seismic wave at the specified point (usually a seismograph station).

Metric System

1 mile = 1.609 kilometers

1 kilometer = 0.6214 mile

1 foot = 0.3048 meter

1 meter = 39.37 inches = 3.281 feet

Selected Bibliography

Albe, E. M. Fournier, "Earthquake!" *UNESCO Courier.* Paris: Atlas World Press Review, 1975.

American Seismology Delegation, "Earthquake Research in China," *Transactions of the American Geophysical Union,* 1975.

W. H. Bakun, et al, "Earthquakes—Can They Be Predicted or Controlled?" *Industrial Research,* Nov. 15, 1974.

Cromie, W. J., "Earthquake early warning," *Science Year 1975.* Chicago: World Book, 1976.

Dempewolff, R. F., and M. McClintock, "Today's forecast: Earthquake," *Popular Mechanics,* December, 1976.

Earthquake Information Bulletin, Published bi-monthly by the U.S. Geological Survey, available from Superintendent of Documents, U.S. Government Printing Office, Washington, D.C. 20402 at $3.00 per year, Volume 8 was published in 1976. Current studies of earthquakes are described in laymen's terms.

Electric Power Research Institute: Applied Nucleonics Company. "Seismic Design of Nuclear Power Plants—An Assessment," Final report, June 1975.

Hass, J. E., and Dennis Mileti, "Socioeconomic Impact of Earthquake Prediction on Government, Business, and Community: Research Findings, Issues, and Implications for Organizational Policy." Boulder, Colorado: University of Colorado, Boulder, (Institute of Behavioral Sciences), 1976.

Iacopi, R., *Earthquake Country,* Menlo Park, California, Lane Books, 1971.

Jaroff, L., "Forecasting the earth's convulsions," *1977 Nature/ Science Annual.* New York: Time-Life Books, 1976.

National Academy of Sciences: Panel on Earthquake Prediction of the Committee on Seismology, "Predicting Earthquakes," *A*

Scientific And Technical Evaluation With Implications For Society. Washington, D.C.: N.A.S., 1976.

Panel on the Public Policy Implications of Earthquake Prediction, *Earthquake Prediction and Public Policy.* Washington, D.C.: National Academy of Sciences, 1975.

Press, F., "Earthquake prediction," *Scientific American,* May 1975.

Richter, C. F., *Elementary Seismology.* San Francisco: W. H. Freeman and Company, 1958.

Time Magazine, Forecast: Earthquake," September 1, 1975.

U.S. Department of Commerce; National Oceanic and Atmospheric Administration Environmental Research Laboratories. "A Study of Earthquake Losses in the San Francisco Bay Area: Data and Analysis, A Report Prepared in 1972 for the Office of Emergency Preparedness." Superintendent of Documents, U.S. Government Printing Office, Washington, D.C., 20402, c/o GPO Bookstore, $2.85.

U.S. Department of Commerce: National Oceanic and Atmospheric Administration Environmental Research Laboratories. "A Study of Earthquake Losses in the Los Angeles, California Area, A Report Prepared in 1973 for the Federal Disaster Assistance Administration Department of Housing and Urban Development." Superintendent of Documents, U.S. Government Printing Office, Washington, D.C., 20402, c/o GOP Bookstore, $3.50.

U.S. Department of Interior: Federal Disaster Assistance Administration. "Safety and Survival in an Earthquake." Superintendent of Documents, U.S. Government Printing Office, Washington, D.C., 20402, c/o GPO Bookstore, 35¢.

U.S. Geological Survey, "Earthquake Prediction—Opportunity to avert disaster," *U.S. Geological Survey* circular 729, 1976.

U.S. Geological Survey: National Earthquake Hazards Reduction Program. *Abnormal Animal Behavior Prior to Earthquakes: Conference One.* Menlo Park, California: U.S.G.S., 1976.

Yanev, P., *Peace of Mind in Earthquake Country.* San Francisco: Chronicle Books, 1974.

U.S. Geological Survey, 1975, "A study of earthquake losses in the Puget Sound, Washington area." U.S. Geol. Survey open-file report 75–375, 298 pp.

U.S. Geological Survey, 1976, "A study of earthquake losses in the Salt Lake City, Utah area." U.S. Geol. Survey open-file report 76–89, 357 pp.

Index